Lessons from
the
Sandbox

Lessons from
the
Sandbox

USING THE 13 GIFTS OF
CHILDHOOD TO REDISCOVER THE
KEYS TO BUSINESS SUCCESS

Dr. Alan Gregerman

CB
CONTEMPORARY BOOKS

Library of Congress Cataloging-in-Publication Data

Gregerman, Alan S.
    Lessons from the sandbox : Using the 13 gifts of childhood to
rediscover the keys to business success / Alan Gregerman.
        p.   cm.
    Includes bibliographical references.
    ISBN 0-8092-2438-0
    1. Success in business.   I. Title: Business success   II. Title.
    HF5386.G765   2000
    650.1—dc21   99-57947
                                                              CIP

Excerpt from *Charlotte's Web* by E. B. White. Copyright © 1952 (renewed 1980) by E. B. White. Reprinted by permission of HarperCollins Publishers. All rights reserved.
Excerpt from *Pippi Longstocking* by Astrid Lindgren, translated by Florence Lamborn, copyright © 1950 by the Viking Press, Inc., renewed copyright © 1978 by Viking Penguin Inc. Used by permission of Viking Penguin, a division of Penguin Putnam Inc.
Excerpt from *The Tortoise and the Hare* copyright © 1984 by Janet Stevens. Reprinted from *The Tortoise and the Hare* by permission of Holiday House, Inc.
Excerpt from *Snowflake Bentley* by Jacqueline Briggs Martin. Text copyright © 1998 by Jacqueline Briggs Martin. Reprinted by permission of Houghton Mifflin Co. All rights reserved.
Excerpt from *Curious George Goes to the Hospital* by H. A. and Margret Rey. Copyright © 1966 by Margret E. Rey and H. A. Rey. Copyright assigned to Houghton Mifflin Company in 1993. Reprinted by permission of Houghton Mifflin Co. All rights reserved.
Excerpt from *Verdi* copyright © 1997 by Janell Cannon, reprinted by permission of Harcourt, Inc.
"Invention" by Shel Silverstein. Copyright © 1974 by Evil Eye Music, Inc. Reprinted by permission of HarperCollins Publishers. All rights reserved.
Excerpt from *The Velveteen Rabbit* copyright © 1922, the estate of Margery Williams, published by William Heinemann Ltd. and used with permission of Egmont Children's Books Limited, London.
Excerpt from *Make Way for the Ducklings* by Robert McCloskey, copyright © 1941, renewed copyright © 1969 by Robert McCloskey. Used by permission of Viking Penguin, a division of Penguin Putnam Inc.

Published by Contemporary Books
A division of NTC/Contemporary Publishing Group, Inc.
4255 West Touhy Avenue, Lincolnwood (Chicago), Illinois 60712-1975 U.S.A.
Copyright © 2000 by Alan Gregerman
Printed in the United States of America
International Standard Book Number: 0-8092-2438-0

00 01 02 03 04 05 LB 18 17 16 15 14 13 12 11 10 9 8 7 6 5 4 3 2

The world of the 1990s and beyond will not belong to "managers" or those who can make the numbers dance. The world will belong to passionate, driven leaders—people who not only have enormous amounts of energy but who can energize those whom they lead.

JACK WELCH

The trick for grown-ups is to make the effort to recapture what we knew automatically as children.

CAROL LAWRENCE

To my mother and father, who always told me how wonderful it was to have children, and really believed that you could learn neat stuff from kids.

To my wife, Lisa, who brings her own special warmth and magic to the wonder, joy, and occasional frustrations of being a parent.

To our children, Sara, Carly, and Noah, who fill each day with magic and continually provide new insights about leadership, strategy, innovation, growth, profitability, dancing up a storm, and just plain having fun.

Contents

Preface

Greetings and welcome to *Lessons from the Sandbox*—a new and very practical guide to business success based on a profoundly simple idea.

In my work with leading corporations, I teach people how to think creatively in order to grow their businesses and improve bottom-line performances. I have found that drawing pictures, going on treasure hunts, building castles, taking things apart, testing the physical properties of a Slinky, playing catch, writing and telling stories, and just plain exploring, questioning, and having fun can be powerful tools for creating winning business strategies as well as generating successful new products and services, and entirely new ways of doing business. Using these means and others like them, our customers have reinvented their industries, identified more than two hundred new and viable service ideas in less than two days, reduced product development cost and time by 75 percent, saved more than $50 million in operating expenses, created higher levels of customer satisfaction at lower cost, earned 30 percent market shares in an overcrowded marketplace, and developed new models of teamwork. In essence, companies benefit from recapturing the curiosity, openness, honesty, wonder, and inventiveness that we all had as small children.

But don't simply take my word for it. Today, companies like Xerox, Compaq, and AutoDesk are tapping the creativity and wisdom of young people in order to develop breakthrough ideas and gain a clear competitive advantage. These firms involve kids as young as seven in efforts to create winning products for the next century. And Hewlett-Packard has focused its new advertising campaign on children as the role model for a company that is committed to inventing. Some leading venture capitalists are even asking kids to review the logic and clarity of new business concepts. Other companies as diverse as Gateway Computers, Coca-Cola, and Dupont are creating positions for "Chief Imagination" and "Chief Learning" officers in order to place greater emphasis on the need for new ways of thinking, learning, and innovating.

It seems as though almost every company is now talking about thinking "out of the box," and a growing number are actually doing something about it. The box office success of the movie *Big* a few years ago, starring Tom Hanks as a child stuck in a man's body who advises a toy company on the best new product ideas, demonstrated interest in (or at least fascination with) this idea.

Current interest in new ways of thinking and working is largely being fueled by dramatic changes going on in the world of business. These changes include rapid advances in technology, changing notions about work itself, the growth of the Internet as a medium for doing business, the emergence of new markets and new sources of competition, the impact of new business arrangements such as strategic alliances, and changing economics and demographics. Complicated times, it seems, demand quick and enlightened thinking.

So why not learn from the people who were never "in a box" to begin with—that's right, from small children? The same little folks who eat with their hands, jump in puddles, constantly ask "What?" and "Why?", have just begun to put words into complete sentences, dance and sing for no reason at all, like to pick up and examine everything an adult refuses to touch, have figured out how to give the dog a new hairstyle, can spot a playground fifteen miles away, and could happily watch the same episode of *Sesame Street* or *Barney* several hundred times. The same little people who are our children, grandchildren, nieces, nephews, neighbors on tricycles, and those adorable trick-or-treaters in the really small costumes. *The same remarkable creatures that we once were.* Unlikely business gurus? Certainly. Inappropriate advisers to leading corporations? Definitely not. This book will show you why.

Lessons from the Sandbox brings together two of the greatest challenges and passions of my life—business consulting and parenthood. During the past fifteen years I have had the privilege and pleasure of working with more than three hundred large corporations, growing firms, and entrepreneurs as they try to reach their business potential. I could not have asked for better opportunities to learn from and partner with so many talented and motivated people and companies. In the past seven years I also have had the privilege and sheer joy of being part of the lives of three remarkable children. At the times of their births I had no idea how much I would learn from them about life, myself, and what it takes to succeed in today's business world.

This book provides a framework for achieving greater success in business and a set of practical skills to get you started. As you read, I hope that you will also grasp the magic of small children—the magic that is possible again in you and your company or organization.

Acknowledgments

It is a pleasure and privilege to thank everyone whose ideas have helped to shape this book and my thinking about the keys to business success.

To our many customers at VENTURE WORKS who have allowed us to partner with them in growing their companies, trying new things, and creating important innovations. You are living proof that combining the talent and dedication of adults with the gifts of childhood is a powerful combination.

To all of the children who have kept me focused on the magic of childhood. Special thanks to our children Sara, Carly, and Noah, who make every day a wonderful journey. To my niece Irina who was the first toddler I really paid much attention to and now has her driver's license and is thinking about colleges; to my nephew Gregory who proved from a very early age that boys were different than girls and now throws a mean curveball as well; and to my Swedish nephews Mark and Felix and niece Alexandra who demonstrate that the magic of childhood crosses oceans and cultures. Thanks also to all the children, families, and teachers in Woodside Park and at Temple Sinai Nursery School who have taught and inspired me.

Very special thanks are due to my sisters Sandy and Helene Gregerman who were certainly two of the main reasons why I had such a happy childhood, and who continue to share their loving and insightful ideas about adulthood, growing up, work, and kidding around.

To many friends and colleagues who have shared their ideas about innovation, business success, and the magic of childhood. Special thanks to Scott and Pam Strehl, Andy and Susan Shapiro, Barbara Friedman, Mark Citron, Karen and Nick Lygizos, Becky Ripley, Virginia Mayer, Jerry Adams, Myra and Harold Sides, Miffy Morgan, Walt Plosila, Bob Chiron, Jordan Lewis, Rudy Lamone, Tom Paci, and Jim Carlton. Many of the best ideas here have resulted from their give-and-take.

Special thanks to John McKnight, my unofficial adviser and mentor at Northwestern University, who taught me how to look at a rather complex world and find the simple and powerful gifts in every one of its inhabitants.

To my agent, Nancy Crossman, who is everything an author could ask for. She not only believed in this book but was truly excited about its value. Her interest, ideas, and encouragement throughout the process of being a first-time author were critical to getting it done and maintaining my generally pleasant demeanor as I also tried to run our business and be a productive member of our family.

To Kara Leverte, my editor at Contemporary Books, who has been an enthusiastic supporter from the start and regularly shares her own lessons from the sandbox. And to the other members of the Contemporary team who have been a real pleasure to work with. Kimberly Soenen, Publicity Manager, deserves special mention for her great energy, enthusiasm, and creativity in helping to publicize this book. Julia Anderson and the editing team have been thoughtful and helpful throughout.

Special thanks to my family who had to endure many long hours of writing and testing ideas, and an occasional missed bedtime story.

Lessons from
the
Sandbox

Introduction

SMALL CHILDREN PROVIDE wonderful insights into making companies more innovative, enthusiastic, thoughtful, focused, fun, caring, *and* profitable.

This book will teach you how to improve your company's bottom-line performance by rediscovering the special talents that we all had as children.

> *Adults are always asking children what they want to be when they grow up—it's because they're looking for ideas.*
>
> PAULA POUNDSTONE

In Search of Business Success

In recent years, companies and their leaders have turned to a wide range of likely and unlikely advisers to help them improve their performance. In addition to a host of consultants, academics from the leading business schools, and peers, they have sought insight from politicians and war heroes, professional athletes and coaches, religious figures, barbarians, and even a lovable bear from Pooh Corner. Are they desperate for answers? Simply confused? Or trying hard to think "out of the box" in the hope that very different ideas, approaches, and contexts will offer the breakthroughs needed to compete in very complicated times?

One thing is clear. After all of the downsizing, reengineering, reinventing, total quality managing, visioning, strategizing, knowledge managing, balanced scorecarding, ERPing (enterprise resource planning), and a host of other very important "-ings," companies are left with a most fundamental and perplexing problem: "How in the world do we actually grow our business?" It turns out that it is a lot easier to get rid of people, plants, equipment, and old products and practices than it is to create successful new products, services, and market opportunities. To paraphrase a few dozen country music songs: "Growing is the hardest thing to do."

If that's the case, why not take a few lessons from small children? After all, they are veritable engines of growth and development who are busy growing every minute of the day. Close your eyes for ten seconds and a toddler will be taller, wider, and likely to need a larger pair of shoes. They will also be smarter, wiser, and more skillful. Small children are unmatched in their abilities to learn quickly, innovate instantly, and process amazing amounts of new information. Not even a Pentium V chip can match their skills. Kids have even figured out how to grow in their sleep, which stands in marked contrast to adults, who often have trouble paying attention (let alone growing) while they're awake. Yet not until children start to speak with some proficiency do we realize how smart they actually are.

It turns out that the world of small children provides a powerful context for explaining why most companies fail to reach their full potentials and how to succeed in business today and in the future. This book will show how companies, their leaders, and their employees can grow their businesses and improve bottom-line performances dramatically by rediscovering how to think and act more like small children and mastering children's innate abilities to play, learn, lead, innovate, and create magical results. Most of us have lost track of these gifts somewhere between the sandbox and the workplace.

Before going any further, consider two concepts essential to this book and the success of companies. The first is the concept of a "gift," though not in the sense of receiving a present from someone. When we were young, we were endowed with a set of wonderful abilities that enabled us to grow, learn, and engage the world around us. They weren't habits we developed or skills we acquired, though the right habits and skills certainly were valuable contributors to our growth and success as we got older. Instead, these were part of our very natures, and they remain part of our natures even though the world around us has often discouraged us from putting them to good use. The following chapters will look closely at these gifts and their great relevance to success in the world of business.

Gift, n. *a special ability or capacity; natural
endowment; talent*

The second concept is of creating "magic," though not in the sense of a magician pulling a rabbit out of a hat or making an elephant and a moving van disappear at the same time. When we were young, we created magic all the time. We did amazing things almost every day and in the process made great breakthroughs that delighted our audiences. Granted, our audiences were most often Mom, Dad, Grandma, Grandpa, and our siblings, but they were only slightly biased in their reactions to our feats.

> **Mag-ic**, n. *the ability to create something that is honest and full of wonder*

In a nutshell, as kids we used our special gifts to create constant magic. If only we could do that again for our customers, colleagues, employees, and shareholders.

Enter the World of Business

Let me play devil's advocate for a minute and suggest that growing a business, whether new or established, is a relatively easy thing to do. All it requires is a clear understanding of the marketplace, great products and services that meet the needs of your customers, a unique and compelling value proposition, the ability to produce your products or deliver your services profitably, skill in getting enough customers to buy your offerings on a regular basis, a knack for consistent and appropriate innovation across all areas of the business, a team of talented and highly motivated people, and enough money to fund the company's growth. It seems like a simple enough equation:

$$\text{business growth} = \text{the right strategy} \\ + \text{ sound execution} \\ + \text{ the right environment}$$

Many companies have figured this formula out. But a surprisingly large number of companies have raised it to a new level of sophistication (i.e., complexity) as they try to compete and prosper in today's global economy. In doing so, they have made business a lot harder than it has to be. Figure 1 shows just how complicated the business world has become, filled with its dizzying array of new or improved concepts, approaches, fads, and initiatives—all intended to support growth and success. These are not bad ideas in their own right, but as the old commercial used to ask: "Is this really any way to run an airline?" I would argue that it isn't. Also, in a world of growing complexity and rapid change where speed and adaptability are essential, it makes sense to find a simpler, faster, and more flexible frame of reference— and one that comes a bit more naturally to those who have to make it happen.

Enter the World of Small Children

Small children are the living, breathing definition of growth. Their equation for growing is also very simple (Figure 2).

$$\text{childhood growth} = \text{living} \\ + \text{ exploring} \\ + \text{ belonging}$$

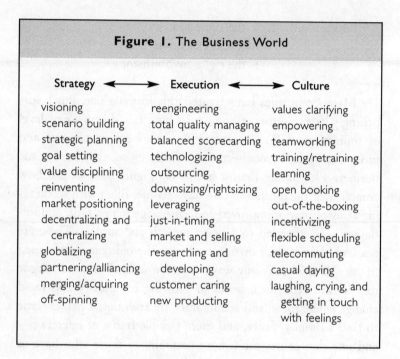

Figure 1. The Business World

Strategy ←——→ Execution ←——→ Culture

Strategy	Execution	Culture
visioning	reengineering	values clarifying
scenario building	total quality managing	empowering
strategic planning	balanced scorecarding	teamworking
goal setting	technologizing	training/retraining
value disciplining	outsourcing	learning
reinventing	downsizing/rightsizing	open booking
market positioning	leveraging	out-of-the-boxing
decentralizing and centralizing	just-in-timing	incentivizing
globalizing	market and selling	flexible scheduling
partnering/alliancing	researching and developing	telecommuting
merging/acquiring	customer caring	casual daying
off-spinning	new producting	laughing, crying, and getting in touch with feelings

Unlike adults, however, small kids haven't figured out how to complicate things. They learn that skill later in life. Instead, small children spend their time living life to the fullest, exploring and learning about everything around them, and trying hard to create comfortable places (or sets of places) in which to belong. Figure 3 shows their world, filled with its straightforward array of natural gifts and inclinations. This was once our world, too, and somewhere inside each of us these gifts and inclinations are available to be rekindled.

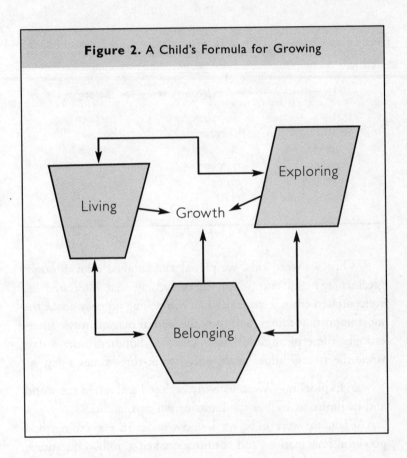

Figure 2. A Child's Formula for Growing

But let's look a bit more closely at how we were when we were small children.

1. **Living**—We engaged the world very differently than most adults do.

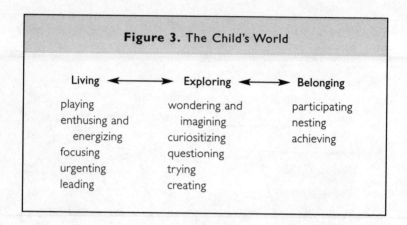

Figure 3. The Child's World

Living ⟷	Exploring ⟷	Belonging
playing	wondering and	participating
enthusing and	imagining	nesting
energizing	curiositizing	achieving
focusing	questioning	
urgenting	trying	
leading	creating	

When we were kids, we played and laughed a lot, brought great energy and enthusiasm to everything that interested us, concentrated when it suited us, had compelling urgency about the most important things, and took the lead in magical ways. Interestingly, the typical child laughs over one hundred times a day, while the average adult laughs only two or three times a day.

2. **Exploring**—We constantly explored and tested the world and its limits, as well as the limits of our own abilities.

When we were kids, we found wonder in everything; had powerful imaginations and curiosities; asked a million questions; created new ideas, connections, and possibilities at the blink of an eye; took calculated risks; and eagerly tried and learned new things whenever the opportunities presented themselves. Between the ages of three and four, most children will learn an average of nine new words a day. That's over three thousand words (i.e., distinct ideas) in a single year.

3. Belonging—We built close relationships and created comfortable and cozy places so we could be at our best.

When we were kids, we looked for opportunities to help out and get involved, made special friendships and relationships—often with people (and creatures) who were very different from us—built strong and safe "nests," set routines, and negotiated effectively the right terms, conditions, and incentives for peak performance. Experts believe that by the age of three, a child's comfort with the world, self-esteem, and sense of belonging are firmly set.

What does all of this mean for the ongoing success of corporations? This simple model of childhood growth and development is a perfect framework for guiding the growth of a company. In fact, practically everything small children do to live, explore, and belong in a very complicated world has clear and profound implications for business performance. Not surprisingly, many successful entrepreneurs seem to instinctively understand this in the early years of their businesses, and capitalize on many of the gifts they had as small children. But established companies lose the knack for growing, just like most adults lose the knack for playing, laughing, innovating, learning, and trying new things.

Look at Figure 3 once more with a slightly different eye. Try to relate these childhood gifts and inclinations to your own business or organization. You might find it helpful to make connections between living and strategy, exploring and execution, and belonging and culture, though there is clearly some overlap. You might also find it helpful to recall the time when you were a child. In both cases, think about what would happen if people in your company were encouraged to play, have more fun at work, explore, try new things, and imagine new universes of opportunities. Or if people took turns in the lead, and everyone was invited (or even required) to question anything and everything in order to make the business better? Or if boundless energy and unbridled enthusiasm filled the offices and halls, and everyone took a real interest in helping their colleagues to succeed? Or if everyone was encouraged to make themselves as "comfortable" as possible in order to do the hard work that had to be done? Or if everyone learned at the speed of light, and growing was the natural order of things?

To make the connection even clearer, consider the similarity of the questions small children and employees in corporations routinely pose:

Children's Questions:	Corporate Questions:
"Why?"	"Why (are we in this mess)?"
"Where are we going?"	"What is our strategy anyway?" (i.e., "Where the hell are we going?")
"Why are we going there?"	"Why the hell are we going there?"
"What are we doing today?"	"What business are we in anyway?"
"What's inside a jellyfish?"	"What is our new product made out of and why isn't it working?"
"Do I have to take a nappy?"	"Do we have to have another meeting to sort things out around here?"
"Why do I have to share?"	"Why do we have to work with the people in marketing?"
"Why doesn't Papa wear a bib for lunch?"	"Why does the chairman's son get all the great projects?"
"Why is that boy crying?"	"Why are so many people unhappy here?"

"Can I paint Papa's face?"

"Are there monsters in the closet?"

"Can I make a brain with Play-Doh?"

"Why can't we have more fun around here?"

"Why is everyone always fighting over turf around here?"

"Does the CEO have Play-Doh for brains?"

In this book you will learn in very practical terms how to apply this model of growth and development to the task of growing your business. In the process, you will also rediscover some amazing talents you had as a child. To make the journey as relevant to your world as possible, the book focuses on thirteen special gifts we all had naturally as small children. They are the gifts of play, enthusiasm and energy, focus, urgency, leadership, wonder, curiosity, questioning, trying, creativity, participation, cozy places, and accomplishment (see Figure 4). Put together, they provide refreshing and powerful insight into corporate success.

The following chapters look at each of these gifts in detail. Each chapter begins with an excerpt from a well-known children's story or poem and a brief "snapshot" about childhood that illustrates each gift, followed by a discussion of the gift and how it applies to the business world. At the end of each chapter, a page called Just for Fun *and* Profit will help you get started in rediscovering how your company can use each gift to improve business results. The concluding chapter ties these gifts together and looks at opportunities for incorporating them into the life of your business. There's even a short "test" at the end to see how you and your company stack up against the lessons presented.

Figure 4. The Thirteen Gifts

1. the gift of play
2. the gift of enthusiasm and energy
3. the gift of focus
4. the gift of urgency
5. the gift of leadership
6. the gift of wonder
7. the gift of curiosity
8. the gift of questioning
9. the gift of trying
10. the gift of creativity
11. the gift of participation
12. the gift of cozy places
13. the gift of accomplishment

You can read this book straight through, a chapter at a time, or any other way you would like to. But you will probably get the most out of it by using it as a companion on a continuing journey to recapture the magic in yourself and your organization. So feel free to read, play, wrestle, wonder, question, and even (God forbid) mark it up! After all, it is not worth the paper it's written on if it doesn't make a difference in your world.

A Note About the Other Side of Small Children

I feel a slight obligation to admit that small children are far from perfect. In fact, there are times when they can drive you absolutely nuts. At their worst, kids can be selfish, self-centered, and stubborn. They can also whine, complain, and say mean things if they don't get their own way. They can disrupt any conversation or activity in which they are not the center of attention. They can be impossible to reason with. They can obscure the truth. They can stall and take forever to do things—especially when it is time for bed. They can get frustrated easily and lose their composure in a split second. They can make an incredible mess out of anything at any time and can even break things of great value. In other words, small children at their worst are a lot like adults at their worst.

Part I

Living

There are three kinds of people in the
   world:
Those who make things happen;
Those who watch things happen;
And those who wonder what happened.

ANONYMOUS

Let's step back to the time when we were two years old. You probably don't recall that time with great clarity, so let's try to refresh your memory.

When we were two, we lived life to the fullest. We played all the time, laughed until it hurt, sang silly songs, learned at the speed of light, and constantly did things that created great excitement for us and everyone around us. We wandered the world with all of our senses turned up high: observing everything in Technicolor, touching everything within reach, climbing on anything our little bodies could get up on, chasing cats and butterflies, following the sounds and smells that caught our attention, and putting most things in our mouths to the great dismay of parents and other caregivers. We even remained active while we were sitting still or lying down: knocking things over, drawing on our clothes and bodies, talking to our stuffed animal friends, and reading books with great interest even though we didn't recognize a single word. If we had older siblings, we probably spent a lot of time following them around and copying their every move and utterance—even the ones we should not have.

When we were small children, great energy, enthusiasm, and passion filled us. We delighted in each new activity and beamed with joy upon mastering any new skill, including hiding large quantities of perishable food products under the sofa cushions. We also felt keen urgency about everything that was really important to us, and had great persistence in getting our needs met.

You might argue that back then we had plenty of free time for leading full lives and engaging the world. After all, we were not constrained by having to go to work. But remember, we were, in fact, constrained to a large degree by our caretakers' schedules and activities. Yet that didn't seem to slow us down at all. We remained focused on our work and our core mission, which was to live, play, and have fun.

Most kids work very hard during the early years of child-hood—only their job is to play. And they don't need to take time off from play (though an occasional nap or time-out is not a bad idea). Most adults, however, work to earn the opportunity to play in their time off. By looking back at the way we lived and engaged the world as young children, we can rediscover how to incorporate play and living life to the fullest into our lives in companies.

Crawling, Running, and Getting Results

It is not uncommon to hear parents boast that their children began to walk at an early age. "She was walking at ten months," colleagues once told me, as if to indicate their child had some amazing talent or gift, or they had passed on some remarkable genes and were by implication also amazing. "Wow!" I responded, "That's fantastic." Of course, I didn't have a particular frame of reference before my wife and I had kids. I have no memory of my own first steps, but have been told that I didn't start walking until I was fifteen months old. I do recall with great fondness that my child-hood nickname was "The Horse" (as in "big, slow, and plodding" *rather than* "walks within hours of birth"), which might help to explain why it took me a few extra months to get on my feet.

But that's OK. I'm doing fine in my forties, and business associates and friends have told me I actually walk pretty well. After all, what was the big rush back then? Crawling was fun. And as we know now, crawling stimulates the brain much more than walking. So when our first child didn't walk until her first birthday, I was not worried. And when her uneasy walking quickly developed into falling down, walking faster, falling down some more, running, falling down some more, and then needing constant adult supervision, my wife and I could draw only one conclusion: this walking stuff was completely overrated. What parent in their right mind would brag about an event that truly marked the end of ever relaxing or having peace of mind? When kids are crawling, parents can still get something else done. When kids start walking, parents better put on running shoes. Forget automobiles, submarines, air travel, hang gliding, or space flight. Learning to walk was, and is, the single most influential and life-altering advance in the history of transportation.

Needless to say, walking turns into running, and running turns into climbing, and each helps to greatly enlarge a child's world. In fact, the early years of childhood are filled with the most significant breakthroughs in our lives. My somewhat-less-than-scientific research suggests fourteen "epic" events (i.e., new skills) that shape the lives of young children. Figure 5 summarizes these in chronological order. Each of these skills enables small children to more effectively capitalize on the childhood gifts covered in this book.

The most important thing about these skills is the fact that kids learn them with great playfulness, energy, enthusiasm, focus,

---

Figure 5. Epic Events in the Life of a Child

sitting up
recognizing that an adult is
    making a silly expression
crawling
standing
falling down
walking
running
climbing
going to the emergency room
talking
discovering your nose
using the potty
reading
telling a bad joke

---

freedom, and urgency, and with a clear sense that there is no time like the present. Having mastered these skills, kids try to take more control of their world, leading everyone they meet on an amazing journey.

When we were kids, we lived life to the fullest by nature.

Many of the critical breakthroughs in the life of a company also occur during its early years. These include:

- coming up with an initial business idea (or breakthrough discovery)
- putting together the funding to get started
- launching the business
- building a team to guide and grow the enterprise
- getting initial customers
- creating excitement in the marketplace
- doing whatever it takes to survive and succeed
- figuring out how to enhance the value provided to customers
- raising additional funding to grow the business

And whether the business is Yahoo, Merck, Crate and Barrel, or the landscaping firm around the corner, these early milestones are approached with great excitement, energy, and a sense of real urgency.

But as businesses grow and mature, the apparent need for structure, discipline, and systems takes hold. And this often includes the hiring of "professional" managers to take over leadership from

> *While we try to teach our children all about life, our children teach us what life is all about.*
>
> ANGELA SCHWINDT

the entrepreneurs who started the company. While many companies strive to maintain the passion of their youth, they find it to be a real struggle. Some, like 3M, seem to do a better job by emphasizing the importance of the entrepreneurial spirit as part of their culture and practices. Others are less successful at recapturing some of the magic and energy they once had and need again in order to innovate consistently and grow.

1

The Gift of Play

To COMPETE SUCCESSFULLY in the future, companies
will need to redefine the nature and content of
work and recognize the importance of play.

The nature and content of work is one of the hottest topics in the world of business today, as companies search for a magic formula to find, motivate, and keep the best employees. But how do we make work consistently meaningful, fun, and productive for everyone in our organization?

Small children are busy working all the time and loving it; only *their* job is to play. The way they play, the results they get, how they avoid boredom, and how they never want to stop "working" offers real insight into the growth and success of companies and organizations. When we were young, we delighted in our day jobs. There is no reason why we can't delight in them again.

The journey is the reward.

STEVEN JOBS, FOUNDER,
APPLE COMPUTER

"Where do you think I'd better go?" "Anywhere you like, anywhere you like," said the goose.

"Go down through the orchard, root up the sod! Go down through the garden, dig up the radishes! Root up everything! Eat grass! Look for corn! Look for oats! Run all over! Skip and dance, jump and prance! Go down through the orchard and stroll in the woods! The world is a wonderful place when you're young."

"I can see that," replied Wilbur. He gave a jump in the air, twirled, ran a few steps, stopped, looked all around, sniffed the smells of afternoon, and then set off walking down through the orchard.

—E. B. WHITE, *CHARLOTTE'S WEB*, 1952

Let's start at the very beginning with the real guts of what it takes to grow and prosper. When we were kids, we spent most of our waking hours playing, which helped to get our brains and bodies working and created lots of opportunities for growth. We crawled, walked, ran, climbed, jumped, swung, danced, sang, laughed, fell, got up, fell again, drooled, burped, made messes, and generally had a great time. We found balls and other things to throw and kick, puddles to sit in, sticks to do neat stuff with, creatures to befriend, games to make up, flowers to pull apart, and bowls full of messy food to put on top of our heads. We spun around in circles until we got really dizzy, and some of us did somersaults by the time we were eighteen months old. We even loved to play as newborns, though this required the encouragement and stimulation of others. And we regularly asked people to tickle us because being tickled was a lot of fun. Our job was to play, and we relished each moment.

Puddle!

Try to imagine you are a small child walking down the street looking for something fun to do when all of a sudden you notice a puddle. It is not just a puddle; it is a really good one—deep, wide, wet, and full of messy stuff. Imagine you are wearing your nicest clothes and a brand-new pair of dress shoes. If you are good at pretending, you will sense very quickly that this could be a magical moment.

When we were small children, a mysterious and wonderful magnetic force drew us to puddles. A giant flashing sign above every puddle (or so it must have seemed) said: "Welcome (your name here)! We are delighted that you have come to visit." With such an invitation, it was no wonder our smiles grew bigger the closer we got. When we were just about to jump into the middle of it, we probably screamed: "Puddle!" with great joy and anticipation. In our world at that time, one word made a perfectly complete sentence.

Simply jumping into a puddle once was not really playing. We needed to experience this wonder of nature in all of its splendor. So after our initial jump, we looked down and adjusted our feet to make sure the water had surrounded us and covered our shoes. Then we wiggled our feet a bit more to get a better sense of how deep the puddle was. Then we made a quick little splash. Then a slightly bigger splash. Then a quick little jump. Then a slightly bigger jump. Then a rapid series of jumps, up and down and side to side. We looked down to admire our pants or dress, socks or tights, legs, and feet, all covered with as much dirty water and guck as possible. Upon seeing the great results of our work, some of us probably stepped back and then ran full speed into the puddle to see just how much water we could displace. Some of us even sat down in the puddle, depending, of course, on how hot it was outside or whether the spirit moved us.

Then, after a great sigh of accomplishment, we headed to the next puddle, knowing full well they always came in pairs and each new puddle brought its own share of excitement and surprises. Maybe they all looked the same to adults. But in the mind of a small child, a puddle found is a puddle earned. When we were kids, we lived, played, and splashed for the moment.

Now let's return to our world as grown-ups and revisit the very same puddle. Only this time, we approach the puddle with the very clear understanding that it is a nuisance to be avoided.

Above the puddle, if you notice it in time, is a giant sign that says, "Beware (your name here)! You have enough trouble to deal with today without stepping in me." With such a warning it is no wonder we would grimace and look for the fastest and driest way around the puddle. If there are other people close by, we might even scream: "Puddle!" as a public service announcement, or even curse it as a pothole and one more reason to question the local government's ability to use our tax dollars wisely.

Most adults go out of their way to avoid puddles. They are not in the least curious about what is inside puddles or how big a splash they can make. A puddle is a potential disruption to the day and an unwanted chance for an unscheduled visit to the dry cleaners. Adults have even invented items of apparel to reduce the impact of stepping in puddles. They call them rain boots, rubbers, or galoshes, and these must seem a bit odd to a small child, who wonders why anyone would want to ruin such a grand experience. The experience of seeing a puddle is even more troubling for parents. After all, they have just dressed the little guy or gal and he or she is about to make a giant mess. Alarms go off, and Mom or Dad race to scoop him or her up before his natural inclinations take over and his clothes and the day are ruined!

When we were small children, we sought out every puddle. As adults we seek to avoid them. When we were kids, we incorporated play into everything we did. As adults we give play a name and most of us make sure it is a distinct part of our lives, separate from the world of work. We set aside time to play games, pursue hobbies, or take vacations, but not time to make play a part of doing a better job at whatever we do. Too many of us view work as something we must do for at least eight hours a day to earn the right to play on our time off. If only we remembered that play is a valuable gift we received at birth and can be used to improve the quality and results of our work lives.

A Small Child's Guide to Play

Before looking more specifically at the value of play in the success of companies, let's briefly look beyond a simple puddle to the workdays of children and adults. Figure 6 presents a day in the life of a typical three-year-old; Figure 7 presents a day in the life of a typical working adult. At first glance, some important things stick out.

Kids' days are filled typically with:

- play and fun
- exercising mind and body
- learning, exploring, and experimenting
- creating stuff and making messes
- countless opportunities for self-expression
- variety and flexibility
- doing important stuff
- time for taking a nap
- marching to their own drums

Adults' days are filled typically with:

- meetings and stress
- little or no time for mind and body
- little time to learn, explore, and experiment
- reviewing stuff and cleaning up messes

Figure 6. A Workday in the Life of a Child

7:15 A.M.   Wakes up and calls out: "Mama-a-a-a! Papa-
a-a-a! Where are you?"

7:18 A.M.   Tinkles.

7:19 A.M.   Climbs back into bed to read.

7:38 A.M.   Exercises in bed—stretches, somersaults, and
a few minutes of headstands.

7:45 A.M.   Goes downstairs to say good morning to
her seventy-five-pound dog. "Bear, my little
sweetie pie, I love you!" Hugs and kisses
follow.

7:50 A.M.   Climbs onto the sofa in the den to join
Barney (already in progress).

8:03 A.M.   Attempts to hide as adults try to put her
clothes on.

8:15 A.M.   Breakfast is served in the kitchen—orange
juice, cereal, toast without the edges, and
banana yogurt. Cereal bowl is turned upside
down on head to get extra attention.

8:43 A.M.   Quickly washes face, brushes most teeth, and
combs hair.

8:59 A.M.   Into the car for the ride to preschool.

9:15 A.M.   Arrives at preschool to begin three hours of
playing, fun, art, and music. Highlight of the
day is collage of pasta, brightly colored
feathers, and cookies.

12:25 P.M.   Home for lunch. Tells Mama: "This is not my
peanut butter day!"

(cont.)

Figure 6. A Workday in the Life of a Child (continued)

1:05 P.M.	Conducts complex kitchen experiments designed to use as many containers and utensils as possible while flooding the kitchen floor. Leaves stuff on the floor.
1:26 P.M.	Goes to neighborhood swimming pool for two hours of wetness and socializing.
3:30 P.M.	Home to nap. Discusses the importance of taking a nap as Mama falls asleep.
4:30 P.M.	Wakes Mama so she can play in the yard.
4:38 P.M.	Yard work interrupted by soccer, hide-and-seek, chasing the dog, playing with worms, and drawing primitive symbols on the driveway with chalk.
5:30 P.M.	Helps to prepare dinner by conducting additional science experiments using as many containers and utensils as possible.
5:43 P.M.	Discusses the relative importance of keeping the laboratory (and kitchen) clean as the table is set.
6:02 P.M.	Mama and Papa clean kitchen floor as dinner is served.
6:09 P.M.	Gets up from the table, carrying some food and wearing the rest, as Mama and Papa sit down for dinner. Spices up dinner conversation with: "I have to go potty."
6:45 P.M.	Family walk in the neighborhood while holding dog on leash. Makes two stops to visit friends and swing on their swings.

Figure 6. A Workday in the Life of a Child (continued)

7:18 P.M.	Bath time. Practices swimming strokes and tests seaworthiness of various objects.
7:45 P.M.	Dries hair, puts on pajamas, brushes teeth and hair, goes potty again.
7:51 P.M.	Picks four new library books to read, then gets into a cozy corner of the bed.
8:20 P.M.	Lights out. Talks about the day. Asks Papa to tell her a story.
8:29 P.M.	Papa falls asleep while telling the story. Keeps "reading" to herself and her stuffed animal friends for another twenty minutes.

- limited opportunities for self-expression
- more of the same
- doing urgent stuff
- beating a drum to get attention

When we were small children, our job description was an open book waiting to be filled with anything we could try, imagine, or stumble onto. In the process, we figured out how our bodies and minds worked, how to communicate and socialize, how to create cool things to do, and how the world around us was organized. If we had been given a job title at the time, it would have probably been Chief Playing Officer, or simply CPO, and we would have been made directly responsible for initiating games

Figure 7. A Workday in the Life of an Adult

6:00 A.M.	Wakes up and calls out: "No, it can't be six o'clock already!"
6:03 A.M.	Stumbles to the bathroom. Tinkles. Stretches for eight seconds.
6:04 A.M.	Splashes face with water. Brushes some teeth. Jumps into the shower.
6:18 A.M.	Gets dressed, combs hair.
6:33 A.M.	Goes downstairs. Turns on the coffee pot. Ponders a world filled with breakfast possibilities. Chooses a bowl of high-fiber bran flakes.
6:35 A.M.	Turns on the radio to hear the traffic and weather report.
6:40 A.M.	Greets the seventy-five-pound dog. "Bear, do you really need a walk this morning? OK, let's go!" Heads out the door with leash and coffee mug in hand.
7:02 A.M.	Finds car keys. Starts car. Turns on the radio to hear the traffic report and then heads off to battle a growing number of hostile commuters.
7:19 A.M.	Stuck in traffic. Tries not to curse at other drivers (who might have guns). Turns off the traffic report.
7:52 A.M.	Arrives at work—stressed, confused, exhausted, and eager to face the day.
7:54 A.M.	Checks E-mail. Eighteen new messages since last night. Replies to top three.

Figure 7. A Workday in the Life of an Adult (continued)

8:00 A.M.	Staff meeting. Gives report on new performance-appraisal system. The applause is deafening.
9:00 A.M.	Meeting on the new phone system. Explains that everyone will need training to reap the anticipated productivity benefits and to just make a basic call.
10:00 A.M.	Meeting on improving marketing and sales effort and its results. Hears the word *focus* eighteen times.
11:55 A.M.	Checks phone messages. Replies to top three. Spouse will have to wait.
12:10 P.M.	Grabs a quick sandwich and a large caffeine-filled beverage.
12:40 P.M.	Impromptu meeting with boss to discuss elusive objectives and how to achieve them with a new sense of vigor.
1:30 P.M.	Interview with job candidate. Asks insightful questions and discusses what makes this an exciting place to work and the benefits of being a self-starter.
2:15 P.M.	Interview with next job candidate. Asks a few questions and discusses what makes this a pretty good place to work and the benefits of being a self-starter.
3:00 P.M.	Interview with the final job candidate. Discusses what makes this a tolerable place to work and the necessity of being a self-starter.

(cont.)

Figure 7. A Workday in the Life of an Adult (continued)

4:00 P.M.	Meeting on improving communication with field staff. Arrives at odd conclusion that some face-to-face interaction might improve morale.
5:45 P.M.	Returns from last meeting to reflect on key strategic objectives. Vows to spend more time thinking about them tomorrow or the next day.
5:52 P.M.	Checks E-mail again. Forty-seven messages. Responds to fourteen that have life-or-death implications.
6:45 P.M.	Heads home—stressed, confused, exhausted, and eager to face the night. Calls spouse from the car.

and exercises, getting people to have fun and laugh, and taking on new and unknown projects.

If there had been clear metrics for evaluating our job performance they would have likely included actual measures of our nonstop mental, physical, and emotional growth, as well as some indicators of our abilities to stir things up and get results. And we would have exceeded all expectations except our own. After all, we loved our jobs and were naturally inclined to work with great energy, skill, and flair. Since we were learning to count and even do addition, we would have even been able to follow along and try to improve our performances based on the management reports and feedback we received.

The Challenge for Companies and Their Leaders

When we were children, we played naturally, joyfully, and constantly. All we needed to have fun was a ball, a rock, a tree, a creek, a dog, some shampoo, some crayons and something to write on, a cup, a bottle of Elmer's glue or some other sticky substance, three feathers from a bird of unknown origin (and unknown cleanliness), or several real or imaginary friends. Most important, all we really needed to do was wake up, get our minds and bodies moving, and engage the world around us. Just being ourselves produced incredible results in learning, innovating, solving problems, getting along, and just plain growing.

> **Play**, v. *to occupy oneself in amusement, sport, or some other activity in which there is an opportunity to have fun, learn something, and make a mess*

By the time we enter the adult world of work, most of us have lost the strong connection between work and play, and many of us have lost the knack for having fun, doing new things, and messing around. For us, work and even learning become serious pursuits that require discipline, structured thinking, and shared methods. We have specific titles, credentials, duties, tasks, schedules, things to get done, and ways to get them done. Under the weight of important priorities, we no longer have time to even smell the flowers, let alone pull them apart. Worse yet, we spend very little time trying to figure out how our bodies and minds work, and how the world around us is organized.

If there are clear metrics for measuring our job performances now, they are probably very specific and likely to be tied to our companies' short-term desires to increase revenues, profits, P/E ratios, ROI, RONA, or any other combination of letters. And some of us exceed the expectations we are given without ever approaching our own full potentials or really helping our companies to reach theirs. The thought that playing could lead to breakthroughs in the ways we do business rarely, if ever, crosses our minds.

There are, of course, a few notable exceptions like Southwest Airlines which incorporates play and humor into its operations and even tries to engage its customers in having fun during flights. And many leading technology firms, as well as businesses in creative fields like advertising and architecture, are designing more playful workplaces that include game rooms, coffee bars, basketball courts, media centers, jogging tracks, and even gardens. In a highly competitive marketplace these companies are trying to make the world of work more dynamic and fun for a new generation of young, talented, and very mobile workers who sign on for 70–80 hours a week and expect to get some exercise and bring their pets to the office.

But most companies view play as something that is separate from the serious business of work. Employees may share a laugh by the coffeepot and post "Dilbert" cartoons on their doors or cubes, but they are expected to get down to business when the workday starts in earnest. The only other times most companies actually plan to have fun together are at annual picnics, holiday parties, the team-building components of retreats, or when employees are part of an after-work bowling team or a softball league.

There are also companies engaged in what has recently been called "serious play" as part of their business practices. These firms, including industry leaders like AT&T, Boeing, Microsoft, and Sony are using simulation games and modeling tools or "toys" to improve their abilities to innovate. It is not exactly what small kids have in mind, but it is a step in the direction of using games, play, and new ways of thinking to get better results.

Take a minute to look closely at your company. Think about the important things that need to get done and the critical issues you face in navigating change. If your company is like most businesses, you probably need to innovate faster and with more skill. You probably need to increase the effectiveness of your marketing and sales efforts so that you stand out in a crowd. You probably need to do a better job of finding, training, motivating, and retaining great employees. You probably need to continue to reduce the cost of doing business. You might even need to improve customer service or strengthen teamwork and morale. And you might need to be better at using technology to support your products, services, and the way you communicate.

Whatever your priorities are, take another minute to think about the role of play in improving your results. At first glance you might see how having more fun could improve teamwork, morale, and spirit in your workplace. But that's just scratching the surface. Remember that kids learn by playing and incorporate play into everything they do. What about developing a game that helps your people improve production or service delivery? What about injecting play and humor into efforts to attract the best employees or energize customer service?

Maybe the right starting point for your company is simply to commit to testing the value of play. Begin by asking people across the organization to identify specific opportunities to interject fun into their work activities and space. Then try some of their ideas. One company we work with started by creating a game room for its employees and set game times when people were encouraged to put down their work and have fun. Another instituted playful days when everyone in the building came to work in costumes, formal attire, or mismatched clothes. Another established a mandatory ten-minute playtime at the start of every meeting. Others have sent their people to nearby playgrounds or even built their own playgrounds. And one company created a Wiffle ball golf course and gave out tee times to employees who needed a break. So use your imagination to come up with practical and fun ideas to change the dynamic of your workplace.

Figure 8 shows some of the things kids do at the playground. These should trigger ideas for things you might decide to do. We know that most people are more likely to leap tall buildings in single bounds when they are being challenged and having fun. Figure 9 suggests some ways to bring the playground into work.

In the Introduction, we set out a formula for growing a child and growing a business that began with a notion of how kids engage the world. The ability to play as a way of living is the first essential building block for growing and reaching our full potential as people and companies.

When we are able to play,

we can imagine worlds of possibilities and opportunities
we can see problems in new and more revealing light
we create a common language for acting, working together,
    and forging real partnerships
we see colleagues as people worth interacting with rather than
    hostile competitors for company resources and promotions

Figure 8. The World of the Playground

Equipment	Games to Play
sandbox	catch
swings	basketball
slide	soccer
seesaw	hide-and-seek
jungle gym	tag
merry-go-round	hopscotch
tunnels	running around
trees	tumbling
benches	leapfrog
water fountains	jump rope
	London Bridge
	badminton
	bowling
	blowing bubbles
	juggling stuff
	drawing chalk pictures
	treasure hunts
	Red Light, Green Light
	wild goose chases

we relieve the stress of day-to-day events and gain the energy
and enthusiasm to do amazing things
we also improve our ability to laugh at our finest mistakes
and applaud our finest accomplishments together
we are free to reinvent the business and gain a lasting competitive edge

Figure 9. The Playground at Work

Physical Places

Build an outdoor playground with all your favorite equipment

Put up some basketball hoops on the wall of your building

Paint lines for hopscotch and other games on the parking lot

Create an indoor playground with your favorite indoor
    equipment

Create an "active" game room with table tennis, pool,
    foosball, air hockey, and other fun stuff

Create a board game room with your favorite games, puzzles,
    brain testers, and some easels for drawing and painting

Set up play areas in the corners of conference/meeting
    rooms

Create a board game library where people can check out
    games to play in their offices or work areas

Build a company Wiffle ball golf course

Some Games to Play

Hopscotch, four-square, dodgeball, hot potato, jump
    rope, etc.

Basketball, soccer, softball, badminton

Pool, Ping-Pong, air hockey, foosball

Chess, checkers, Monopoly, Pictionary, Risk

Designing and flying paper airplanes

Drawing, painting

Playing musical instruments

Puzzles

Wiffle golf

Big Lesson #1

You can only do really good work if you enjoy what you are doing.

Summary

In a small child's world, playing is a way of working and living. When we were kids, we grew by creating games, having fun, making messes, and getting so completely dirty that new detergents had to be invented. As adults in companies, we should look for puddles to jump in and other opportunities to make play a key part of our formula for success.

> *Play is often talked about as if it were a relief from learning. But for children play is serious learning. Play is really the work of childhood.*
>
> FRED ROGERS (MR. ROGERS)

Lessons from the Sandbox

Play

- You can only do really good work if you enjoy what you are doing.

- Make play a valued part of every day.

- Create games that help you to improve your work results.

- Use your mind and your body, and get them to help each other.

- Laugh at least a hundred times a day.

- Never pass up an opportunity to jump in a puddle or make a major mess.

Just for Fun *and* Profit

Here are some things you can do today to rediscover the gift of play in order to improve your company or business unit's bottom-line success.

Visit a Playground

Take your colleagues or team members on a field trip to a local playground to rediscover how small children work. Take some mental notes about the nature of play and how kids engage the world around them. Then think about their relevance to your world of work. While you're out there, spend at least a few minutes swinging, sliding, or playing hopscotch. But make sure to stretch before you start.

Take Stock of Your Commitment to Play

Now make a log of your workday that records how much time you devote to playing, having fun, and actually engaging the world around you. Then note the number of times you and your colleagues laugh. Use this "inventory" as a baseline for redefining the role of play and fun in your performance.

Make Time to Play and Have Fun

Block out at least fifteen minutes during each workday to play and have fun. Fill this time with one of your favorite playtime activities. Throw a ball or a Frisbee, go to a playground, learn to juggle, shoot hoops, build a puzzle, draw, paint, doodle, sing, dance, stretch, take a hike, or do anything else that gets your mind and body moving in a different way. Just get up and have some fun! The simple act of doing this will stimulate your brain and enhance your spirit and productivity.

2

The Gift of Enthusiasm and Energy

To COMPETE SUCCESSFULLY in the future, companies will need to create an even greater sense of enthusiasm and energy for their customers, employees, and shareholders.

Every company is looking for ways to make itself stand out from the pack. What they often forget is the ongoing importance of maintaining their enthusiasm, energy, and passion. Small children are great ambassadors for anything worth doing. What excites them, how they show their enthusiasm, and their levels of energy and determination offer real insight for the growth and success of companies and organizations. When we were young, we were passionate about every assignment we took on. There is no reason why we can't be passionate about our work again.

The real secret of success is enthusiasm.

WALTER CHRYSLER, FOUNDER,
CHRYSLER MOTORS

"Pippi heated a big kettle of water and without more ado poured it out on the kitchen floor. She took off her big shoes and laid them neatly on the bread plate. She tied two scrubbing brushes on her bare feet and skated over the floor, plowing through the water so that it splashed all around her.

"I certainly should have been a skating princess," she said and kicked her left foot up so high that the scrubbing brush broke a piece out of the overhead light.

"Grace and charm I have at least," she continued and skipped nimbly over a chair standing in her way.

"Well, now I guess it's clean," she said at last and took off the brushes.

—ASTRID LINDGREN, *PIPPI
LONGSTOCKING*, 1950

When we were kids, we were bundles of energy and enthusiasm, buzzing around from one interesting thing to the next. We were always looking for new sources of excitement. At the slightest mention of anything that seemed worth doing—i.e., anything fun, new, or that offered a chance to learn a skill—we would jump up instantly, grab our shoes and at least one dirty sock, and head straight for the door with giant smiles on our faces. Things that adults often viewed as necessities of life, we viewed as golden opportunities to learn, innovate, and grow.

Somersault!

During the thirty seconds between my second and third somersaults, I realized with great certainty that I was no longer a kid, and that any thought I had entertained of still competing in the Olympics was unrealistic at best. Even the new and seemingly less strenuous Olympic events like ballroom dancing, bowling, synchronized walking, Velcro archery, air hockey, and small-parcel delivery—events in which some of the participants looked silly and out of shape—were now out of reach. So when a group of three four-year-olds each completed 25 consecutive somersaults without stopping to catch their breath (or their bearings), I knew something had changed in my physical makeup and required adjustment. When they decided to play hide-and-seek and several versions of tag nonstop for the next hour, screaming at the top of their lungs and laughing the entire time, I knew my adult notions of enthusiasm and energy had been greatly reduced by the passage of time. Sure, I wanted to keep up. Sure, I could recall the joys of these games. Sure, their enthusiasm was contagious. But let's be realistic (or "get real," as kids would say).

It wasn't just the kind of hide-and-seek that we used to play in the house on a rainy day—where a good hiding place was either behind the nearest sofa or in the broom closet. It was the run-as-fast-as-you-can-to-the-next-county version, complete with crawling under park benches and climbing up in trees and diving into long-forgotten piles of leaves. Fortunately, roughly twenty seconds after small children arrive at the perfect hiding places, boredom sets in and they abruptly announce their whereabouts to the unsuspecting pursuers. But that only adds to the excitement.

Research indicates that most adults think they have a lot of energy. They can go to work, find a place to eat lunch, come home, mow the lawn, coach soccer, sprint to the curb with the recyclables, and even surf the Web. But how many of us can do twenty-five somersaults in a row without coming up for air, or play a game that requires running around like crazy for an hour without stopping? In fact, after my third somersault I was so dizzy that I was certain my brain had gone through a major reorganization and possibly a downsizing. At least professional athletes take a time-out to gather their thoughts and catch their breath. Kids don't stop until sometime after the lights are turned out and everyone says good night.

A Small Child's Guide to Energy and Enthusiasm

When we were small kids, we had natural inclinations to be energetic and enthusiastic about practically anything that interested us. It wasn't just somersaults or games in the park. We dove headfirst into everything possible. We marveled at new things, delighted in our favorite familiar things, and constantly tried to master new skills and get involved in other people's stuff. We also sought out opportunities to be given more responsibility, like fixing breakfast or walking a dog three times our size on a street filled with potential predators.

En-thu-si-asm, n. *rapturous interest, excitement, or zeal that is contagious if not treated*

As kids, even the smallest things excited us:

"Would you like to play in the park?" Mom might have asked.
"Sure!"
"Will you help me make pancakes for breakfast?" Dad might have inquired.
"I'd love to!"
"Should we read a new book?"
"Perfect!"
"Want to go to the store and maybe get an ice cream?"
"Ye-e-s! Ye-e-s! Ye-e-s!"
"Will you come with me to return books to the library?"
"Great!"
"Can you help take out the garbage?"
"Definitely!"
"Shall we work on an art project?"
"When can we start?"
"Want to go to the zoo?"
"You're the best mother/father in history!"

"Can you clean up the mess in your room?"
"Do I have to?" (Even enthusiasm has its limits.)

We even showed our enthusiasm and energy by the way we walked or ran, moving across any terrain with a style that was all our own. We weren't even trying to be cool. And we weren't always trying to be careful. Our minds and bodies simply worked together in response to a world filled with interesting and exciting things to participate in. So what if we looked like a duck trying to take off? When we saw someone special—like Mom, Dad, Grandma, Grandpa, or a favorite cousin—we would run full speed to greet them. Try to remember the last time you ran at any speed as an adult to greet someone. It certainly doesn't happen very often in the world of business (unless we are late to meet one of our investors at the airport or we spot a big customer with a large check on the day we have to make payroll). In fact, except for romantic movies, TV commercials about beer, and the world track-and-field championships, adults rarely run to greet anyone.

We also used our enthusiasm to create additional opportunities to do new things. "Can I help you do that?" was our common refrain from the moment we could put six words together. It was always said with big smiles and a metric ton of persistence. When the response was: "Not right now, I'm doing something that isn't really for kids" (i.e., something that involves the use of sharp implements, breakable objects, power tools, or toxic chemicals), we quickly looked for something else to enthuse our way into, asking several hundred times: "Well, can I help you do something else?" until the answer was a resounding "Sure."

We even asked for help in enthusiastic ways: "Will you read this great book to me?" "Will you help me to put my shoes on backward?" "Will you give me a giant push so I can swing way up in the sky?" "Will you teach me to paint like Monet?" or, "Will you help me to collect a bunch of silly bugs and then launch them into space?" Questions filled with such passion were hard for our parents to say no to. And while we were in the middle of something fun, we made sure to communicate our excitement by saying (quite naturally) things like, "Can we do it again?" "This is the most beautiful flower ever!" "Look, it's purple! That's my most favorite color in the whole world!" "I love going on the swing!" "Can we paint just one more picture?" or simply, "Wow!" When we were small children, a very high percentage of the things we said ended with exclamation marks.

En-er-gy, n. *vitality and intensity of expression in living life and engaging the world*

Through it all, there was always a great constant in the way that we engaged the world around us. Our enthusiasm, energy, passion, and sense of joy were completely honest, truthful, and sincere.

The Challenge for Companies and Their Leaders

Enthusiasm and energy are absolutely essential for building anything of value. Yet most companies generally lack both today. Walk through the halls of almost any business (except a high-

Figure 10. A Child's Guide to Enthusiasm and Energy

Things That Are Worthy of Enthusiasm and Energy

anything new
anything familiar that is fun
anything that involves learning a new skill
anything that involves helping and participating
anything that involves a higher level of responsibility
anything that involves getting to play with an animal

Things That Are Not Worthy of Enthusiasm and Energy

anything that is boring
anything that is too scary
anything that is too hard to do alone

some examples:

- cleaning your room
- washing your hair (and getting soap in your eyes)
- eating broccoli
- going to sleep before you want to
- having to sit quietly while other people are talking

flying start-up filled with dreams of greatness and going public quickly) and you are likely to find very few signs of real excitement and passion. There may be pockets of people who enthusiastically make great products, serve customers with great care, and work on the next great breakthroughs, but for the most part, people just do their jobs while watching the clock. Too many people approach their jobs as hired hands who would work for someone else tomorrow if the price were right, and too many businesses assume that very little can be done about it. As a result, too few people and companies really live up to their potentials.

Everyone knows that the start of any new venture is filled with great energy, passion, and promise. When you're long on ideas and short on customers, capital, and people to help you to implement them, you better do whatever it takes to create a landslide of interest and excitement. And usually that's not a problem. If you have given up a well-paying job and put up your home as collateral, you must believe that your "widget on a chip" is the greatest thing since self-toasting bread—possibly even the next Microsoft. So you should be able to get totally psyched up about your product's remarkable elegance and the value it will provide to potential customers. In fact, you and your marketing person (to the extent that you have one) are probably so passionate that you can make initial orders come in, investors appear, and actually find a merry band of people who want to be part of your team. Things go along swimmingly as long as the business does well, cash flow is positive, and there are stock options left to distribute.

But somewhere along the way, most companies lose their driving sense of enthusiasm and excitement. And when they do, how can they expect all of their stakeholders and the marketplace to stay excited?

Imagine how much more successful your company would be if most of your people were truly enthusiastic about your business and what it had to offer. And what if most of your people were eager not only to do somersaults for your customers but also to do them for each other? Let's think back to what excited us as small children so we can rediscover what can and should excite us as grown-ups at work. Remember we were drawn to things that

- were new
- were familiar but fun
- involved learning a new skill
- involved real participation
- involved a higher level of responsibility

But they had to be things that *we really believed were worth doing*.

So our starting points for enhancing enthusiasm and energy should be those things that make us special as companies and not only are worth doing but are worth getting excited about. Let's call this our "unique value proposition." It's what sets us apart. We don't have to be great at everything. But we do have to be great, or willing to try to be great, at something of real value that is tied closely to our vision of how we intend to grow our business. Is it the amazing commitment to our customers? Is it the high quality of our products or services? Is it our unconditional guarantees of customer satisfaction? Is it our world-class technical support? Is it our abilities to use technology more effectively than anyone else in meeting the needs of our customers? Is it our strong commitment to enabling all of our employees to balance their work and personal lives? Or is it simply the fact that we sell unique products, including a new breakfast cereal that contains the perfect amounts of all four basic food groups and tastes exactly like Godiva chocolate? Whatever it is that we commit to hanging our hat on, it must be something worth doing and worth doing well. (See Figure 11.)

It doesn't mean that we have to provide the latest and greatest products or services, or that we have to create a cure for an intractable disease. As long as we do something of real value, we have the basis for building enthusiasm. Look at Finland's SOL Cleaning Service, a fast growing and very dynamic commercial cleaning company. In an industry known for poor service, minimal job satisfaction, and high employee turnover, SOL is using fun, freedom, and autonomy to create high levels of enthusiasm and commitment among both its employees and customers.

And there are plenty of other examples of companies that create excitement and energy in established industries by focusing on the customer's real bottom-line. Think about Michelin's TV commercials with beautiful babies riding across wet pavement on top of tires. They never tell you that Michelin tires are thicker or stronger or last longer. They simply emphasize that "so much is riding on your tires." It's not a question of buying the best tire, but rather a gut issue of protecting your loved ones. And if that is not worthy of passion and enthusiasm, what is?

Building real enthusiasm and energy about something worth doing—i.e., our unique value propositions—gives us a clear advantage in attracting and retaining the best people, finding and keeping the right customers, getting attention in the marketplace and inside our own organizations, raising money, moving an important product or project forward, standing out from the crowd, or reinventing our industries.

Enthusiasm and energy must start at the top of companies, where leaders set the tone for what is valued and possible. From

Figure 11. A Corporate Guide to Enthusiasm and Energy

Things That Are Worthy of Enthusiasm and Energy

our customers and partners
our employees
our vision and strategy
our products and services
new ideas
our shareholders, investors, and other financial backers
anything that involves learning a new skill

Things That Are Not Worthy of Enthusiasm and Energy

anything that is boring and cannot be made fun
anything that we are afraid or unwilling to dedicate our
    resources to
anything that we are not committed to doing well
anything that does not help us to achieve our vision and
    strategy

some examples:

- going through our in-box and "to do" list
- attending meetings that have no clear purpose or objective
- working on projects that lack real commitment
- eating broccoli

there, companies must commit to helping all of their people have a clear sense of what sets the organization apart and their roles in making it happen. As leaders, we need to help everyone understand how to make their jobs worth doing and fun. This means giving them the guidance, encouragement, tools, and freedom to figure out ways they can improve their own performances in support of key business objectives, and thus make the most of their jobs. And we need to continually look for new people with the passion and energy we all had as children.

Big Lesson #2

Enthusiasm about something worth doing is powerful, contagious, and essential.

Summary

For small children, enthusiasm and energy are the best ways to engage a world filled with countless opportunities. Kids understand innately that there is great power in purposeful enthusiasm and doing a million somersaults on a perfect summer day. As adults in companies, we should see that the power of doing flips is more than simply stirring up our brains.

> *The secret of genius is to carry the spirit of the child into old age, which means never losing your enthusiasm.*
>
> — ALDOUS HUXLEY

Lessons from the Sandbox

Enthusiasm and Energy

- Enthusiasm about something worth doing is powerful, contagious, and essential.

- Anything that provides real value is worth doing well.

- Having a lot of enthusiasm and energy can help get attention and create new opportunities.

- Always let people know when you are excited to see them.

- Never do a somersault on a full stomach.

Just for Fun *and* Profit

Here are some things you can do today to rediscover the gift of enthusiasm and energy in order to improve your company's or business unit's bottom-line success.

Look at Some of Your Childhood Pictures

Start by looking through some pictures or home movies of you as a small child. Pull out a bunch that show your enthusiasm and energy in action. Think about what you were doing at the time and how you were doing it. Were you playing, singing, having a party, working on a project, or taking a family trip? Then make a few notes (in your mind or on a piece of paper) about how you interacted with the world when you were young. Compare that with today and think about the value of those gifts now in the world of work. You might also want to put some of these pictures up in your office.

Spend a Day with a Small Child

Plan a day with a small child and try to get a sense of how he or she engages the world. Go for a walk around the neighborhood, play catch or hide-and-seek, go to a playground or a museum, share a pizza, or just hang out. As you are doing this, pay close attention to what excites the child and the energy exuded when having fun.

Have an Enthusiasm Day at Work

Ask people to come into work with something they are enthusiastic about. It can be something at work, a hobby, an accomplishment, a prized possession, or their dog or cat. Then, have everyone talk about what it takes to be consistently enthusiastic. Write their ideas down and think about how these ideas translate into the world of work and into bringing more energy and passion into your business in particular.

3

The Gift of Focus

To COMPETE SUCCESSFULLY in the future, companies will need to know where they are going and how they intend to get there. They will also need to ask the right questions along the way.

Companies spend a lot of time, money, and energy developing vision statements, mission statements, and strategies to guide their growth. But all this effort rarely helps them to develop focused and flexible plans for engaging the world around them and learning to navigate in changing seas.

Small children provide a strong reminder that vision and strategy are not documents produced with great fanfare and then left on a shelf. They are the living, breathing, and changing guides for getting someplace special—on a journey to a place where everyone wants to go.

One of my most important jobs is keeping the company focused on our core values and on the business that we want to exploit.

MEG WHITMAN, CEO, EBAY INC.

Wynken, Blynken, and Nod one night
Sailed off in a wooden shoe—
Sailed on a river of crystal light,
Into a sea of dew.

"Where are you going, and what do you wish?"
The old moon asked the three.
"We have come to fish for the herring fish
That live in this beautiful sea;
Nets of silver and gold have we!"
Said Wynken,
Blynken,
And Nod.

EUGENE FIELD, *POEMS OF CHILDHOOD*, 1894

If you have ever taken a car trip with small children, or have ever been a kid on a car trip, you probably have very clear memories of the experience. They probably include making up games, singing silly songs, telling "knock-knock" jokes, eating plenty of sticky food, stopping for countless bathroom breaks, and counting red cars and license plates from distant lands like Ohio, Louisiana, and Montana. But there is really a lot more to it, as I rediscovered a few years ago.

"Are We Yawst?"

It must have been very clear to Sara that we had been retracing the same ground for the last thirty minutes; because three hours into our two-hour drive to visit friends on the east coast of Sweden, she suddenly let out the painful question, "Papa, are we yawst?" with all the passion of someone whose small bottom and smaller attention span were wearing a bit thin. And, as any self-respecting male would have done, I quickly responded to allay her fears: "No, sweetheart, we're not lost. We know exactly where we're going. We just don't know exactly how to get there!"

That wasn't good enough for a three-year-old. "I think we are yawst!" she replied from her car seat of judgment, surveying the rainy, foggy, and unfamiliar landscape with new intensity. "We are very, very yawst!" Then, after a moment of less than quiet reflection, she asked: "Where are we going anyway?"

"We are going to spend a few days on a little island with Maria, Staffan, and their family," I answered, hoping that knowledge of our destination might ease her concern. "But why are we going there, Papa?" Sara persisted. "Because they have three kids to play with, rocks to climb on, a forest to hide in, puddles to jump in, and if we are lucky we can even go swimming, ride in a boat, fish, and maybe toast marshmallows." As you might guess, that was a much better answer to give a small child held captive in a Volvo for close to an eternity, and she instantly smiled and said: "Yippie! When will we be there?"

But a few moments later her anticipated joy lapsed back into frustration. She turned to Mama and asked, "Are we yawst?" followed closely by, "I think we are very, very, very yawst!" Mama responded, quickly and unconvincingly: "Don't worry, sweetheart, we're not really lost. Papa is great with directions. Besides, he has two degrees in geography from leading Big Ten universities." The last comment was a hopeful attempt to score points with someone who had no idea what the word *geography* meant, let alone the notion of a "university." To her credit, Sara did know that the word *big* often had positive connotations and the number *ten* was well within her grasp, though she failed to see their connection as a single phrase.

"We are yawst, Mama!" she continued. "I know we are." "Don't worry," Mama replied, "we'll be there any minute now. Who wants to sing a song or play a game until we get there?" "I don't want to play another game. I just want to get there now," a tired and increasingly angry child called back.

Just then Sara spotted a young woman riding a bicycle. "Maybe she can tell us how to get to the island, Papa!" "Not a bad idea," I replied, continuing to drive straight ahead as the rain came down harder. "Papa, can we ask her?" At that moment Mama decided to share one of the great lessons in life. "You might as well know now," she began, as violins played a sad tune somewhere off in the distance, "your father is a guy, and guys are genetically incapable of asking for directions."

On this point she was definitely right, but I was part of a long history of men who wouldn't ask for directions: Christopher Columbus, yawst looking for India; Richard Nixon, yawst using a tape recorder; and Moses, the yawstest guy of them all—yawst in a relatively small desert for forty years. He wouldn't even ask a nomad how to get to Mount Sinai. What harm would it have done?

Ten minutes later we finally pulled up to our friends. As they stood waving in the rain (and checking their watches), I heard grateful applause and a suddenly happy little voice exclaim, "We are found! Mama and Papa, we are found!" followed by, "Good job, Papa! We did it!"

"Thanks, sweetheart," I replied, freed from the wrath of the world's smallest backseat driver.

A Small Child's Guide to Vision, Strategy, and Focus

Left to their own devices, small children may choose to wander without a final stop in mind. But they become keenly focused on where the ship is going when someone else is guiding it. When we were small kids, we had a clear, compelling, constant, and very rational desire to know (and try to influence) our destinations. Within seconds of beginning any journey, we were likely to start asking four essential questions:

1. "Where are we going?"

2. "Why are we going there?"

3. "How do we get there?"

4. "When will we arrive?"

From a practical standpoint, these questions helped us get in the right frame of mind for a trip and decide what things to bring along. After all, what sensible person would go anywhere without taking along a bunch of special friends (i.e., our favorite stuffed and live animals, dolls, or trucks); our favorite books, toys, games, and music; some crayons and something to write on; at least one of our softest blankets; and a variety of snacks that could permanently attach to upholstery?

These questions also served to ensure that we always remained focused on the objective. It also didn't hurt, in terms of focus at least, that we asked them close to a million times before we arrived at the destination. This was especially true of the question dreaded most by parents driving cars: "When will we be there?" closely followed by its nagging friends, "Are we almost there?" and "Are we there yet?" These words have probably made many a parent give up driving entirely. My best response now is to simply say, "We will be there in fifteen minutes if you don't ask ever again and three days if you do." Surprisingly, this answer is pretty effective even with six-year-olds.

Fo-cus, n. *a center of intense interest that one cannot easily be distracted from*

But the upside is the fact that once small children focus on something that they want to happen or need to know, they have trouble getting it off their minds. And they keep everyone else focused as well, whether they like it or not.

The Challenge for Companies and Their Leaders

It turns out that *where*, *why*, *how*, and *when* are key questions to ask of any important journey, whether it involves taking a family vacation or trying to guide the growth of a corporation. Yet over the years, I have either observed or been asked to advise dozens of companies that were taking, in essence, the very same trip to a small island off the coast of somewhere they had never been to before. They all began with an idea of where they were going, thought they knew the reason why, claimed to have a clear and correct strategy for getting there, and believed everyone was excited to go along on the journey. (See Figure 12.) But somewhere along the way they got very, very yawst.

In recent years it has become extremely common, if not fashionable, for companies to hold executive retreats and undertake major strategic-planning initiatives to help them decide the right direction to take in this rapidly changing world. At their best, these efforts provide a strong and focused beginning to the ongoing process of strategy, by forcing companies to wrestle with the issues of where, why, how, and when. That's just the starting point. These questions present quickly moving targets in today's and tomorrow's environments. So while we might be clever enough to see where the marketplace is heading right now, it is really hard to see more than two or three years into the future. In many indus-

Figure 12. Things to Take Along on a Trip

In the Car

special friends
our favorite books
some toys and games
plenty of music
crayons and something to write on or an Etch-a-Sketch
a soft blanket and a pillow
lots of snacks and beverages that are not too messy
a good map
a cell phone

When Guiding a Business

the right people
the right knowledge and information
some toys and games
just enough music
a comfortable chair
lots of snacks and beverages that contain caffeine
a good and flexible map
an effective means of communication

tries an awful lot can happen and change in a matter of months. This means strategy must not only keep pace but evolve, and we must continually check our positions, knowledge, and actions against the changing picture of where we are trying to go. And if we intend to succeed in the longer term by actually reinventing our industries and ourselves, even more work must be done.

Also, companies and leaders must have renewed vision, purpose, urgency, openness, and humility, and a consistent willingness to listen to the folks in the backseat when they suggest asking for help. The era of knowing it all (and getting everyone else to come along for the ride) is over. Let's summarize the key ingredients in navigating a company in changing seas:

strategy = the ongoing process of asking
"where?"
(Our best understanding of the future market
and our place in it.)

+

"why?"
(A compelling reason to make the journey.)

+

"how?"
(The roadmap for getting there, including the
competencies we will need to succeed.)

+

"when?"
(A timeline for making it happen and a means
to measure our progress along the way.)

+

a willingness to ask for help

Unfortunately, too many companies and leaders view strategy as either the "adult daily minimum vitamin requirement" for guiding a business or some secret formula for success known only to the most senior executives. In their minds, the task is simple. Take a few "key" people off-site for a few days, plan the perfect attack, and then march confidently into battle. As a result, companies with flawed strategies, or no real strategies at all, head into the market every day, led by leaders who are completely convinced they are going in the right direction and don't need any help at all. Is it any wonder that employees hesitate to call out from the backseat and ask, "Where are we going, anyway?" "Why are we going there?" and "What can we do to help?" After all, it would definitely be a CLM—i.e., career limiting move—in most organizations.

Worse still, many leaders circle their wagons at the slightest hint of concern, arguing even more strongly that their articulated strategy should be clear and inspiring to everyone. Only then do the employees and other shareholders start to question management decisions and suggest that the bosses are clueless (or that "the emperor has no clothes"). And everyone hopes and prays that the new-product-development department will somehow "discover" a rich new continent they can call India or the marketing and sales team will somehow reach Mount Sinai before a revolt or, more likely, a downsizing. And no one goes anywhere near a tape recorder. If only leaders knew that it is more important to ask the right questions than to have all the answers.

In failing to commit to a clear vision and strategy, companies lose the critical focus required to really excel in their businesses. As strange as it might seem, the more focused we are, the easier we can innovate and grow, assuming there is a big enough market opportunity in our chosen products or services. The right focus makes clear to everyone what is needed to build our businesses.

When we were young, we would never have tolerated the lack of vision, strategy, and focus found in many corporations. Taking a trip posed too many obvious concerns. If we had been asked, we would have known that it is better to start an important journey when the direction is crystal clear and everyone is eager to go. If it wasn't clear, we would have asked our leaders to explain their choices of destination—unless, of course, we were going to the zoo, a playground, to Grandma and Grandpa's house, or another one of our favorite places.

When we were small children, we also would have communicated openly and honestly, and probably would have been more willing to ask for help and accept advice when we got stuck along the way. We would have helped each other prepare for the trip if it meant getting there sooner, and we would have encouraged everyone to bring friends, refreshments, and supplies. We might have even suggested that everyone have their own copies of the map to chart their roles and continually measure our progress together—fine-tuning our actions as we got smarter or as the world around us changed. And after a lot of backseat driving, we would have shown appreciation during the journey and started the chorus of applause as soon as we arrived at the destination.

Big Lesson #3

It is important to know where you are going and why you want to go there.

Summary

It is essential for small children to know where they're going and why, and it is just as important for companies. Vision is the important place we choose to go. Strategy is the way we intend to get there. Focus is what keeps us on track. We can work out the details together in the car.

I always wanted to be somebody, but I should have been more specific.

LILY TOMLIN

Lessons from the Sandbox

Vision, Strategy, and Focus

- It is important to know where you are going and why you want to go there.

- Having a clear focus makes it easier to reach our goal.

- Make sure to ask for directions as soon as you get lost.

- Communicating clearly is the best way to keep everyone working together.

- Always show your appreciation when you reach your destination.

- Never underestimate the insight of a small backseat driver.

Just for Fun *and* Profit

Here are some things you can do today to rediscover the gift of focus in order to improve your company's or business unit's bottom-line success.

Take a Trip to a Distant Land

When we were kids, we used to imagine traveling to faraway places where we would have great adventures, discover new things, and make new friends. We can play the same game to improve our understanding of business strategy. All we need is a globe (or a map of the world) and our imagination. Spin the globe with your eyes closed and then point to a spot. Now that you know where you're going, plan your journey. Begin by answering the questions *why*, *how*, and *when*. Then try to figure out what you should bring on the trip and what competencies you will need on the way and once you get there. When you're done, think about how this exercise relates to getting your business or unit to its destination. This can be done on your own or as a team.

Picture This

Draw a picture of the world of your business or unit to get a better understanding of the forces that are influencing your strategy. Look inside the organization first and then at the world around you to identify opportunities and barriers to success. You can do this with your colleagues and then share and discuss your pictures.

Ask for Directions

Do you really understand your company's strategy? If not, ask your boss in a nice way to explain where you are going and why.

4

The Gift of Urgency

To compete successfully in the future, companies will need to keep their eyes on the clock.

The time frames of business become more compressed every day. To succeed, companies must have a clear sense of urgency and a compelling desire and ability to beat the clock. After all, technology is changing faster than our abilities to embrace it and the world is filled with plenty of very hungry competitors. Standing still for just a moment means falling behind.

Small children are driven by definite priorities, short attention spans, stomachs connected directly to brains, and very small bladders. In their world, time is of the essence, and they remind us that we should never delay in getting the really important things done.

We have to be competitive twenty-four hours a day, 365 days a year, or else we will lose business. A sense of urgency about communicating and solving problems is imperative.

MICHAEL DELL, CHAIRMAN AND CEO,
DELL COMPUTER

Suddenly, Hare woke up because the crowd was cheering.

"Yay, Tortoise," the crowd roared.

Tortoise was two steps away from the finish line.

"Slow down, you bowlegged reptile," screamed Hare as he tried to catch up.

But it was too late. Tortoise crossed the line just before the tornado of dust and fur that was Hare flew by. Tortoise had won the race. Hare couldn't believe it.

That measly shell on legs had beaten him.

AN AESOP FABLE, AS ADAPTED BY
JANET STEVENS, 1984

Before we leave the subject of car trips altogether, consider one more essential feature of going anywhere as a small child: the need to pull off the road less than a minute after you have just gotten back in the car. When we were small children, we were often overcome with great fits of urgency.

I'm Going to Explode!

It's six-thirty at night on the Thursday of a holiday weekend, and you and your family are on the way to visit cousins in Ann Arbor, Buffalo, Visalia, or Houston. After almost an hour of looking for a reasonable dining opportunity, Mom and Dad have finally found a place to eat just off exit 37 of the turnpike, or the "highway" if you lived in a part of the world without turnpikes (or the "E6" if you lived in northern Europe). The place is named Kousin Karl's Kountry Kitchen, which should make anyone wonder if they can kook as well as they can spell. Better still, a big handwritten sign in the front window proudly states: "We put gravy on everything!" While your parents' better judgment suggests driving until a fast-food restaurant with a well-known brand name (and consistently mediocre food from the outer reaches of the food pyramid) appears, the little guy or gal in the backseat is so desperate for food that one must strike while the deep fryer is hot.

So you pull off and walk in, quickly capture a booth, and ask the waiter or waitress what is fast and good, with a clear emphasis on *fast*. You learn that they have all manner of fine American cuisine, including burgers, dogs, fried chicken, chicken-fried steak, chipped beef on toast, french fries, chili, spaghetti and meatballs, mashed potatoes, and the like. You realize that the only item you would put gravy on is the mashed potatoes. Nonetheless, you order a bunch of stuff, including milkshakes for everyone, and try to wait patiently for the chef to work his magic.

In a few minutes the food arrives and all hands race for the ketchup. This will be a meal to remember. But the food is actually edible, give or take a handful of maximum strength Tums. And after twenty-five furious minutes of snarfing, spilling, conducting scientific experiments using packets of sugar, salt, pepper, and a bottle of ketchup, the referee steps in to announce the two-minute warning. In 120 seconds you need to be hitting the road if you intend to reach your cousins' house (spelled with a *c*) before Y3K. "This is the last chance to finish your dinner," Mom announces with great fanfare.

As the check arrives, everyone is asked whether or not they need to go to the bathroom. Mom and Dad are the only ones who raise their hands. Rarely do small children have to go to the bathroom right after a meal, especially when they're on a car trip. Nonetheless, the question is asked once more just to be sure. Again, the kids are fine. Then a brief stop to fill the car up with gas. "Last chance for a bathroom," Dad announces. "We're OK," is the reply. Ready to rock and roll.

So everyone climbs back into the car and heads back onto the turnpike, barely noticing a giant sign, "Next exit 78 miles." No problem, just filled the tank, and with a little luck everyone but the driver will be taking a nap very soon. But less than a minute later—i.e., 53 seconds to be exact, but who's counting?—a small voice from the backseat proclaims, "I have to go to the bathroom."

"You do?" Dad responds.

"Yes, I really, really have to go!"

"But we just left the restaurant *and* the gas station and you said that you didn't need to go."

"I didn't need to go then, but I really, really have to go now!"

"But we can't stop now, there's no bathroom here in the middle of the highway."

"I'm going to explode if we don't find a bathroom!"

"Can you hold it at all?"

"No, I'm really going to burst!"

So you pull off onto the shoulder of the highway to find an appropriate shrub.

A Small Child's Guide to Urgency

Urgency is a powerful force in the life of small children. It often sneaks up on them with very little warning, triggered by a strong physical or psychological need that requires immediate attention. Urgency in a kid's world can rarely be planned for. Otherwise, far fewer cars would ever have to pull off the road for food or a bathroom break. Urgent situations compel kids to act quickly and decisively in order to get their needs met, often with behavior that is less than perfectly rational. The following were urgencies to us as small children:

- the need for food
- the need to go potty
- the need for a bear, doll, or security blanket
- the need for Mom (or occasionally Dad)
- the need for a Band-Aid, an ice pack, or a higher form of medical attention

- the need for sleep
- the need for help when cookies are tossed
- the need to crush a younger sibling for messing with our stuff

These things caused real "gut" reactions in us and threatened our ability to live life as we wanted to. They rendered us helpless, pathetic, and unable to focus on all of our other special gifts.

When a small child says he has to go potty, it doesn't mean he is going to grab the newspaper and go upstairs to casually do his business and reflect on the day's events. Rather, his body has sounded the alarm that his relatively short digestive tract is about to burst but has willingly given him fifteen seconds of notice. Similarly, when a small child says she has a tummy ache, it doesn't mean she is thinking about whether or not to eat Italian or Thai food for dinner and would like to discuss the options. It means that she needs food now and any delay will almost instantly turn this precious little angel into Grumpy, Whiney, the Wicked Witch of the Mid-Atlantic, and that disgusting guy in the *Friday the Thirteenth* movies, all rolled into one. When a small child desperately needs his or her mother, no other human being on this or any other planet will suffice (nine months of letting someone do cartwheels inside one's body ought to count for something). In each of these instances, note that the clock isn't simply ticking—it's flying!

Ur-gen-cy, n. *the condition of needing to do something very important so you won't explode*

Some urgent things are not readily recognized by small children. The most obvious ones are the need for sleep or a time-out.

For some strange reason small children are oblivious to all of the signals they send out of the imminent demise of their personalities when they become tired. Someone else must quickly scoop up what is left of the child and find a quiet place to unwind. Whoever coined the phrase, "Never underestimate the value of a good night's sleep (or a nap)," obviously was thinking about small kids.

As children get older, however, they become more skilled at anticipating some of these important urgencies. They also begin to recognize that a slight bit of planning can help avoid some emergencies.

But there are powerful pluses to a child's sense of urgency. First, small children are only urgent about things critical to their well-being. Sure, they make it seem like everything is urgent and can quite often be heard saying things like: "I just have to go outside to play in the snow this minute!" or "I need to ride my bicycle now!" or "We have to read a book right away!" or "If I don't have a bubble bath right now, the dirt will never come off!" But a little friendly discussion, a bit of timely distraction, some basic negotiating, or a bribe can put off these concerns. The response, "Would you rather have an ice cream or take a bubble bath?" usually ends all concern about competing for the Nobel Prize in personal hygiene (though cleanliness should be somewhere just after food, beverages, shelter, and security).

Notice the need for "friendly" rather than "rational" discussion when trying to sort the urgent from the less-than-urgent with kids. Rational discourse is impossible with a small child, just as it is with most domesticated animals and many adults. But often, something about irrational thinking and behavior is essential to appreciating and responding quickly to important things. This brings us to the other critical fact about small children and urgency. Kids are relentless in addressing their urgent needs. From their perspectives, they have no choice. In their minds these situations can only be ignored at great peril. These situations must not only be dealt with but resolved, so life and play (i.e., work) can go on.

The Challenge for Companies and Their Leaders

In the business world, urgent situations are common events. Deadlines sneak up on us; in-boxes fill; crises occur, calling for quick reaction; presumed new opportunities present themselves; and competitors and customers challenge us to change and improve. Yet most companies and the individuals and teams in them spend most of their time dealing with things unessential to their ongoing success. They battle the details without addressing the big picture. Often, they do this because they lack a clear focus and keen sense—rational or otherwise—of what the really important things are. They also find it far easier and more expedient to tackle the little things that are big nuisances than the big things that are hard to get a handle on. As a result, too many people and companies live by long "to do" lists tied to short-term results, rather than a short list of the really important things that will ensure long-term success. When we were kids, we knew to do the important things with compelling urgency and thoughtfulness. As adults we are prone to forget.

We need to assume that urgency around the essential things (see Figure 13) is part of any business today and in the future. To do otherwise puts us at great risk of losing touch with changing markets and customers and failing to react in time. When we were small kids, we had no clue that an urgent event was coming. As companies we need to do our homework so we can anticipate as many urgencies as possible. This means keeping our ears to the ground as well as to the future. To do this, we must keep in constant touch with our customers, employees, partners, and the marketplace just in case important changes in their worlds affect ours. We can't assume that just because we asked if everything was OK a minute ago (or a month ago), it is still OK today. We must also be ready to react to the essential things we cannot foresee. Sometimes we win in business by planning carefully for things; other times we win by reacting more quickly to our guts or by simply making the right new things happen.

The business world is filled with companies that failed to anticipate changes going on around them. It is also filled with companies that seized the day and were nimble enough to re-create themselves and their industries in several split seconds. Think about AOL; it began as a pioneer in the on-line revolution before the Internet emerged as a truly public medium. But a changing environment would force it to redefine its business model. Today it is truly a leader in the broader worlds of interactive services, Web technology, and E-commerce. At its core now is an Internet brand and marketing powerhouse with 20 million subscribers and a growing global reach.

Other companies have capitalized on the importance of urgency. These include firms like FedEx, Airborne, and UPS that have compressed the time frame for doing business and serving

---

Figure 13. Things to Be Urgent About in Business

the need to satisfy the right customers
the need to have a clear direction
the need to have the right people in place
the need to inspire our people to leap the right tall
    buildings in single bounds
the need to pay attention to key changes in our
    marketplace and the world around us
the need for appropriate innovation
the need to work together effectively
the need for help when we screw up big time
the need to do everything faster and better

---

customers. They also include companies like Kinko's that have rewritten the rules for office services by putting twenty-four-hour-a-day support just around the corner from America's small businesses.

Yet understanding the things that are essential for sustaining our lives as growing businesses isn't enough. We also need to think constantly about how to beat the clock in the day-to-day lives of our companies. We need to figure out how to do everything important instantly. For example,

how to produce the best products and services in the shortest
    possible time

how to make needed changes in what we offer, as quickly as
   possible
how to hire and train the best people at the drop of a hat
how to provide instant customer service
how to adapt the latest technology to our operations faster
   than anyone else
how to communicate instantly to all of our people when they
   need to know something important in order to act with
   one clear voice

To succeed and grow, companies must

- have a compelling sense of urgency
- know what is important and requires urgent thinking
  and action
- act decisively to address the important stuff
- give employees a clear sense of what should be urgent
  and why
- create a beat-the-clock mind-set

> *Childhood is that wonderful time*
> *when all you need to do to lose weight*
> *is take a bath.*
>
> JOE MOORE

Big Lesson #4

Matters of the greatest importance require urgency and persistence.

Summary

Small children approach the really important things with unwavering urgency and persistence. Urgent is the name we should only give to essential matters of well-being, growth, and business success, knowing that most things are not truly urgent. And knowing that most things on a menu don't need gravy.

Lessons from the Sandbox

Urgency

- Matters of the greatest importance require urgency and persistence.

- Most things are not that important.

- If it is worth doing, it is worth doing better and faster.

- Whenever possible, it is better to anticipate the future than to be surprised by it.

- Always be prepared to stop on a dime.

- Be cautious of places that put gravy on everything.

Just for Fun *and* Profit

Here are some things you can do today to rediscover the gift of urgency in order to improve your company's or business unit's bottom-line success.

Rethink About Urgency

Take fifteen minutes to write down all of the urgent things on your plate. Now make a list of the essential things your company needs to do to grow and prosper. Compare the lists to see if you are focusing on the right things. Then start to move the unessential items off your "to do" list.

Do Something Important Faster and Better

Pick something important that you are responsible for, and commit to figuring out how to do it faster and better. A good place to start is by looking closely at how you currently do things and questioning each key element until you identify real opportunities to raise the bar. With these opportunities before you, pretend you are a child with an upset stomach and let your compelling sense of urgency take over. How can you improve your performance? How can you reduce the time required by half? How can you get the right people involved? This can be done on your own or as a team.

Spend an Afternoon with a Small Child

Hang out with a small child just before dinnertime to see how he or she reacts to something important and urgent. See if you notice the warning signs, then apply that knowledge to the workplace.

5

The Gift of Leadership

To compete successfully in the future, companies will need leaders who create environments in which real magic can happen.

L eadership is the single most important determinant of business success. Leaders create the environment and set the tone and direction for what is valued, rewarded, and possible. But what does it really take to be an effective leader in these complicated times?

Small children are natural leaders. They know how to get attention and take the lead in simple and wonderful ways—without right or wrong, hidden agendas, passing judgment, or unrealistic expectations. Children bring fresh ideas about how to get everyone in the "organization" to excel by encouraging, supporting, and appreciating their special talents.

Leaders owe a covenant to the corporation or institution, which is, after all, a group of people. Leaders owe the organization a new reference point for what caring, purposeful, committed people can be in the institutional setting.

MAX DE PREE, CHAIRMAN EMERITUS,
HERMAN MILLER

The grand old Duke of York
He had ten thousand men
He marched them up to the top of the hill
And he marched them down again
And when they were up they were up
And when they were down they were down
And when they were only half-way up
They were neither up nor down!

"THE GRAND OLD DUKE OF YORK"
(AN OLD NURSERY RHYME)

One of my clearest recollections of childhood was the occasional Saturday evening when my parents would have friends over for dinner and my sisters and I would have to make way for an adult get-together. I remember the early baths, the Swanson TV dinners—fried chicken with mashed potatoes, corn, and an apple thing in the middle—and putting on our best pajamas so we would be presentable for the few moments when we got to say hello. I also remember hearing the sounds of adults talking and laughing as we tried to fall asleep upstairs, and how we would sneak into the hallway to listen to what they were saying. What do adults talk about when there aren't any kids around? Could they possibly be having fun? To answer these questions we'll have to go back to our childhood and crash the party.

Let's Do It Now!

She walks down the stairs and through the doorway into a crowded room, wearing her nicest pink pajamas, purple velvet slippers, and a somewhat shy grin punctuated by two large dimples. Without making a sound, she captures everyone's attention, then she shyly returns their looks of amusement. In a matter of seconds, all eyes are focused on her as conversations end abruptly, cups and plates are placed quickly and securely on tables, pins are heard dropping softly to the floor, coughs and sneezes are suppressed, trains of thought pull out of their stations, and pets and insects of all types, sizes, and dispositions become motionless. It seems that everyone and everything have stopped to watch her every move, measure her every step, and listen to her every word in the hope of gaining the slightest clue to her intentions. Then, for a split second she stops as well, to collect her thoughts and plan her next move.

Now in the center of the room, she formally greets the crowd with a welcoming smile as if to say, Who are you guys, and what are all of you doing here in my living room? Apparently, Mom and Dad are having a party, and it doesn't take a two-and-a-half-year-old long to figure out that this room full of friends and strangers provides a golden opportunity to put off the dreaded arrival of bedtime and accomplish something of value.

Then, without warning, she does a quick somersault across the middle of the floor. Then another, and another, and still another—her feet finally landing against the side of the coffee table. Everyone gasps as a giant grin breaks out across her face. "That was funny!" she roars, picking herself up from the floor. "I love to do flip-a-dips! They're so much fun!" Then, catching her breath, she asks, "Who wants to flip-a-dip with me?" This was not, of course, meant to be a rhetorical question. "They must need time to warm up," she tells herself. Then, sensing everyone's apprehension about flipping in public, she climbs up onto the sofa, takes off her slippers, and surrounds herself with two large pillows. Then, just as quickly, she climbs back down and says, "I'll be right back. I need to get something." In less than thirty seconds she returns with a very soft blanket, a couple of her favorite stuffed animals, and a bunch of books.

It takes a few moments to arrange everything in just the right way—with a pillow on each side, an animal under each arm, and all ten toes under the blanket—but this is time very well spent in the mind of a little girl. Now set, she lets out a quiet sigh of near-perfect contentment and exclaims: "This is a cozy place! I love to be in a cozy place!" As a chorus of smiles fills the room, she asks softly, "Who will read a book for me?"

"I will!" says the forty-something man at the end of the sofa. "I will, too," says the woman standing by the fireplace. "I'd love to," says a close family friend sitting in the big soft chair. In a matter of seconds, practically everyone has volunteered. "Let's read ten books!" the girl shouts with joy, "or twenty!"

Then the reading begins as a shy and distinguished-looking gentleman sits down beside her. "Can I read the first book to you?" he asks. "I'd like that," the girl replies. "Do you want to be in a cozy place with me?" she wonders aloud. "That would be just perfect for me," he responds. "Oκ, then put your feet under this blanket and we can read *Curious George.*" He starts right into it with lots of enthusiasm and flair. "You are a very good reader," the girl declares. "Thank you," he answers back. "I don't get to read to small kids very often, but I like to read." Soon *Goodnight Moon, Mad About Madeline, Babar, The Runaway Bunny,* and *Mufaro's Beautiful Daughters* have all been read and just about everyone has had the chance to participate. And she has made time to thank them all.

"I love parties," the girl concludes as her mom and dad carry her up to sleep. Much has been accomplished, new friends have been made, bedtime has been kept away, and the essence of leadership has been revealed.

A Small Child's Guide to Leadership

When we were small children, we were natural leaders, getting attention when we entered the room, welcoming people, making sure everyone was comfortable, making clear what needed to be done, getting everyone involved, and encouraging them to do things great and small that really made a difference. We were masters at working a room and creating a context for action.

As small kids we took the lead in wonderful ways, without hidden agendas, passing judgment on people and ideas, or setting unrealistic expectations, but with intentions that were always honest, honorable, and obvious. We took for granted that everyone could participate and that everyone wanted to make a contribution if we knew how to bring out the best in them.

Whether out of desire, necessity, or merely invention, small children know how to get and keep everyone's attention. It's clearly not by the power of their position, but through the gentle and amusing force of their personalities and the sheer strength of their wills. Kids have a real gift for setting the right tone. That's not to say they are always at their best when it is time to take charge. But they are pretty good at learning that one is more likely to get others to come along by relying on warmth, spontaneity, sheer exuberance, confidence, and a clear and compelling plan. And when children aren't at their best, a well-timed nap is often the key to maintaining their leadership edge.

When we were young, we knew how to communicate with great skill. All we needed were a few well-chosen words, a tug on someone's hand, a quick glance in any direction, or a book or game that we could drop in someone's lap. We also knew instinctively how to make each and every person feel at ease. In our world it was easy to create a comfort zone where inhibitions were checked at the door, no one had any limits, and each person could bring his own special abilities to the forefront, and there was always room to share a book under a very soft blanket. In a broader world filled with uncertainty, stress, and discomfort, we found ways to create safe and "cozy places" for ourselves and others where we could all perform at our best.

> **Lead-er-ship**, n. *the ability to get people to leap tall buildings in single bounds and read a children's book aloud at the same time*

As small children we also knew how to be caring cheerleaders, and could break down most barriers with a smile or the simple words, "Good job!" and "Thank you!" For us, encouragement was not a scarce commodity to be parceled out only for superhuman effort. We delighted in giving positive reinforcement (partially because we liked to receive it), and had the knack for building people's self-esteem. We even went out of our way to give people credit for the positive things they did and rarely took credit for things we hadn't done ourselves. As little kids we measured success as a willingness to participate, to take a chance, and the desire to give a part of yourself to the effort at hand. We instinctively knew that if we aren't encouraged to try, we will never take the risk to try again and someday excel. In our world, kindness and gratitude were the currencies of choice.

The Challenge for Companies and Their Leaders

We often view corporate leaders with the same awe, trepidation, and wonder that we have toward small children. When they walk into a crowded room, we all come to attention, hoping their words and actions will reassure and inspire us. Instead, we often end up holding our breaths and waiting to see what gets knocked off the table or spilled in our laps, or what other messes we will have to clean up before the end of the day. Granted, it's not an easy job guiding a company. But so many leaders seem to miss the basics.

Leadership is, first and foremost, about creating a place in which magic can happen. We should expect our leaders to challenge us to be our best, to learn and grow, and to reinvent our businesses. After all, leadership is about what is possible. But it has to begin with getting and keeping everyone's attention in clear and positive ways. Whether that means wearing pink pajamas and purple slippers, doing flip-a-dips at a staff meeting, or having an inspiring game plan for ensuring the future, leaders need to turn heads, capture imaginations, set agendas, keep focus, and create compelling reasons for people to get on board and take initiative. That doesn't mean we should expect our leaders to have all the answers. But we should expect them to ask most of the right questions, like "Who will read a book for me?" or "Who wants to be in a cozy place?" or "Who wants to take the initiative to make something important happen for our company?" We also expect our leaders to be honest, open, enthusiastic, and decisive.

Leadership includes being willing to keep people informed about what is really going on and the desire to give people guidance so they can make a real difference. Too often, leaders hide or obscure the truth in order to maintain control or in the hope that problems will simply go away. If small kids ran companies, everyone would have the natural inclination to communicate openly and honestly. After all, it's impossible for small children to keep secrets, and it's pretty difficult to obscure the truth without knowing a lot of big words. Everyone would be reading out of the same book, sharing the same information, and trying hard to take turns with the tools needed to color, cut, and paste the next chapters.

If companies were run by small children, leaders would be visible and accessible facilitators of good and important things. They would manage by walking *and* talking around, taking sincere interest in the organization's direction and all of their people, and creating safe places for nurturing new ideas. And it would all be easy and fun to do. For small kids, discomfort with sitting still gives them a distinct advantage over adults. By nature, they walk around and check out everything. After all, everything new is fun and cool, so why not visit with people in the organization to find out what they are working on? As leaders kids would also seek advice, give advice, and place the greatest value on everyone's special talents. In a small child's world, we are judged by our abilities and not our limitations.

We need leaders in companies who are both ardent cheerleaders and kind and supportive critics, knowing innately that the most amazing growth occurs when we seek to challenge, encourage, give positive reinforcement, and build self-esteem. Magic happens at all levels of companies and organizations. The best leaders are the ones who create an environment where the most magic can happen.

Big Lesson #5

Leaders create the context in which real magic happens.

Summary

It takes at least two to share a book. Leaders aren't always in the lead; they just make sure that good things happen. Real leaders have the rare ability to get any of us to read silly books out loud in a room full of friends and strangers.

> *Any kid will run an errand for you if you ask at bedtime.*
>
> RED SKELTON

Lessons from the Sandbox

Leadership

- Leaders create the context in which real magic happens.

- Leaders get everyone's attention.

- Leaders capture people's imaginations about what is possible and what needs to be done.

- Leaders give everyone an important part to play and guidance and encouragement to succeed.

- Leaders are decisive but are careful not take themselves too seriously.

- Leaders wear their best pajamas when they are expecting important guests.

Just for Fun *and* Profit

Here are some things you can do today to rediscover the gift of leadership in order to improve your company's or business unit's bottom-line performance.

Take a Look at Your Approach to Leadership

Compare your approach to leadership now with your approach as a small child. How have you changed the way you get people to participate in making important things happen? Then think about the ways you can incorporate a child's natural gift for leading into your role.

Involve People in New Ways

Test your leadership skills by getting people in your organization to do something fun that is not in their job descriptions. You might start by getting everyone on your team to read a book out loud. Or you might enlist their involvement in a volunteer activity tied to a cause you believe in that might relate to your particular business, such as improving literacy. In either case, test your ability to get attention and create interest and excitement.

Communicate Too Well

Commit to making your communication as clear and open as possible. You will be quite surprised at how important this can be in motivating people and how effective it is as a tool for keeping everyone focused and reducing the level of gossip and confusion.

Part II

Exploring

When one tugs at a single thing in nature,
he finds it attached to the rest of the
world.

JOHN MUIR

Now that we're starting to think like kids again, let's turn our attention to the second part of our formula for growing: the way we explored, collected, and tested information about the world around us.

When we were small children, we relentlessly explored everything around us. From our vantage point, the world was a continuous parade of miracles gladly unfolding before our eyes and our hands at just the slightest prompting. We were filled with powerful wonder, imagination, and curiosity and were not content until we had pulled ideas and things apart, examined them in detail (which often included putting them in our mouths), and left what remained in a pile behind us. We marveled at the moon and the stars and their likely inhabitants but also found uncharted worlds beneath a single fallen leaf. We also asked a million questions about everything we discovered, partly because it was a great way to learn and partly because it was fun to get attention and keep adults on their toes. We also tried everything we could, including broccoli and brussels sprouts, knowing innately that if we didn't try new things, we would never grow to our full potential. In the process, we created new ideas and inventions by making new connections and developing our keen propensity for innovation.

When we were small children, our minds were like sponges, absorbing incredible amounts of information every minute of every day. You might argue that we had a big advantage then. After all, our minds were open books. We didn't know much to begin with, so everything around us was there for the learning, and we took it all in with great skill and delight. We could, however, make the same argument now as adults, except for the open book part. Almost everything around us is there for the learning today. Although we know a lot of stuff (about our jobs, our hobbies, our friends and relatives, where we live, and the news we choose to read), it is a very small fraction of what we could learn. And we use a relatively small percentage of our brains to do it. In fact, research suggests that the typical adult uses roughly one percent of his or her brain. To make it sound better, that is about two hundred million brain cells—out of twenty billion. Also, while we are always learning new things, we have become relatively slower learners and even slower adapters of new ideas. So it becomes even more interesting and relevant to think back to our childhoods to gain insight into how to learn more effectively.

One of the key themes in business today is learning and the importance of managing knowledge and creating learning organizations. Yet we are trying to do this without playing to our greatest strength—the hidden ability to learn at the speed of life, which is there for us to recapture. Kids learn differently and with far greater skill than do adults, largely because they are open to learning everything and do not pass judgment on what is worth learning and what is not. Also, kids learn with an eye toward action. They are constantly busy doing things to either learn more or apply their learning. Their mode of learning is exploration, and they do it in a number of important ways.

Talar Du Engelska?

It is not uncommon to hear adults in the United States acknowledge their desires to speak another language. I certainly share this sentiment. After all, people in other countries go to great lengths to communicate with us, and an amazingly large number now speak English fluently. I must admit, however, that the decision to make English the international language was met with great joy by myself and most of my closest friends and business associates. It isn't that English is the most beautiful language. I could listen to French for hours at a time without knowing what it meant, simply imagining that people were speaking about food, wine, fashion, style, the arts, or love. And I'm sure that English is not the most grammatical or logical. That distinction, I was told at a party, belongs to Klingon—the language of Star Trek (and spoken by my father when I was young).

But the truth is that English, with all its character flaws, is the only language I have any reasonable level of proficiency in after forty-some years on the planet. I am somewhat embarrassed (to put it mildly) that I am so poor at learning other people's languages. I applaud everyone who is proficient in a second language. I tried Spanish in high school and college, but was not the brightest lamp on the language porch (although recently I have overheard and understood parts of some remarkable conversations on elevators). I tell people I am just plain bad at learning languages, as though that is a good excuse for my linguistic transgressions. But it's just an excuse, and whenever I travel abroad I feel guilty.

So it is poetic justice that I would marry someone from another country, with a difficult language to learn. And, at the risk of offending those with roots in Scandinavia, I admit I am slowly learning to speak Swedish. Swedish is a perfectly reasonable language with a long and illustrious history. It is also a language spoken by only ten million people in the world, roughly

80 percent of whom seem to speak English fluently. So I'm not doing it because it is the perfect second language.

But why do I mention this as we begin to look at the role of exploration and how small children learn? Because, quite simply (and amazingly to me at least), our two-year-old daughter now understands and speaks English and Swedish as though they both come to her naturally. Furthermore, she has never complained of any difficulty in learning either one.

Experts acknowledge that it is much easier for kids to learn new languages. But why? My guess is that kids truly are sponges for most learning, welcoming new stuff with great passion and soaking up as much as they can. They also haven't been trained to think in one particular way or pass judgment on what is worth learning and what isn't. Why not try to take in anything the world has to offer—especially when it will help you to communicate with small kids in faraway places? Of course, children have learning strengths and weaknesses at an early age. But they often seem to work around them with far better results than most adults are able to get.

For Swedish speakers, or those simply curious as we move toward the chapter on curiosity, Figure (Figur) 14 presents the 13 childhood gifts in this great language.

> *I am not young enough to know everything.*
>
> OSCAR WILDE

Figur 14. De Tretton Gåvorna

1. gåvan av lek
2. gåvan av entusiasm och energi
3. gåvan av inriktning
4. gåvan av angelägenhet
5. gåvan av ledarskap
6. gåvan av under
7. gåvan av kuriositet
8. gåvan av ifrågasättning
9. gåvan av ansträngning
10. gåvan av kreation
11. gåvan av deltagande
12. gåvan av mysiga ställen
13. gåvan av utförande

6

The Gift of Wonder

To compete successfully in the future, companies will need to find wonder and possibilities in both the big picture and details of business life.

Companies and their leaders often talk about reinventing their businesses, rethinking their products and services, creating new markets, and shifting paradigms as the means to grow and prosper. Yet rarely do they commit to actually thinking differently in order to imagine truly new worlds filled with possibilities and opportunities.

Small children live in a world where everything is amazing and full of wonder. They remind us that we will never reach our full potential if we aren't willing to dream and dare to make bold dreams come true.

*All our dreams can come true—if we
have the courage to pursue them.*

WALT DISNEY, FOUNDER,
DISNEY STUDIOS

Willie Bentley's happiest days were snowstorm days.

He watched snowflakes fall on his mittens,

on the dried grass of Vermont farm fields,

on the dark metal handle of the barn door.

He said snow was as beautiful as butterflies,

or apple blossoms.

JACQUELINE BRIGGS MARTIN,
SNOWFLAKE BENTLEY, 1998

Remember the first time you saw snowflakes coming down, a rainbow stretching across the sky, a hummingbird hovering in flight, a brightly-colored flower, an airplane, a puppy, a circus clown, or someone selling cotton candy. They were, no doubt, moments filled with wonder. "What is this?" you might have said, with a voice conveying your sheer amazement at one of countless miracles unfolding before your eyes. Practically every new experience we had as small children (at least, the positive ones) was a miraculous event, and each day brought further proof that anything was possible.

This Is the Best Snow in History!

One cold and perfect morning in December, a four-year-old boy looked out the window at a sky filled with snowflakes and knew instantly that it was a day to make magical friends in the snow. "Can we make a snowman?" he asked, just barely wiping the sleep from his eyes. "That would be great!" his parents answered. "But first we have to have some breakfast and put on our snow clothes so we won't catch colds." "Ok," said the boy, as he raced to his closet and pulled out his winter boots from the pile of clothes, toys, and miscellaneous stuff. Then down the hall he went, looking for his snowsuit, ski cap, and mittens. "Not so fast," said Mom, "there's a bowl of cereal on the table just waiting to be eaten." "Is it 'Super Sweet and Disgusting Orange Bonker Bits'" he asked, hoping to avoid the less appealing options. "Your favorite, and I can make you a cup of hot chocolate, too." "To take outside?" "Ok." After all, the snow was calling, and who was he to keep it waiting?

Within seconds of reaching the front yard, the boy began collecting snow to build the body for a snowman. "This is the best snow in history!" he shouted, as his parents came out to join the fun. "We need a hat and a scarf," he continued, sprinting back to the doorway to check out the supply. "I'll get a carrot for the nose," said Mom, as she headed back to the kitchen at a somewhat slower pace. "And the eyes?" the boy asked, surveying the snow-covered ground for ideas. "Maybe some stones, or some buttons from the sewing table," his dad suggested. "Perfect!" Twigs for arms would make the final touch. In a matter of minutes, the snowman was done.

The small boy looked at the snowman with wonder and pride. His parents smiled joyfully, seeing his happiness and possibly acknowledging that they too recalled the wonder of childhood. Then they began heading back to the house. But the boy's work wasn't done yet.

"Can we make a snowwoman, too?" the boy asked. "I think he needs a friend when we go in the house." "Sure," said Mom with a look of mild delight. "And a snowboy and a snowgirl? And a snow puppy dog and a snow kitty cat?" "Sure we can, and we can even make a snow alligator," continued the dad, caught up in the excitement of the moment. "Let's do it now!" the boy exclaimed. "I love snow more than anything in the whole world!" So Dad headed back in the house to get a thermos of hot chocolate and the green food coloring necessary to create a perfect snow alligator with perfect snow.

Snow is still a wonder to me after all these winters of shoveling, falling on the frozen pavement, and digging and scraping to get the car out of the driveway. One of the great and recurring miracles of the year, snow is one of my reasons for not wanting to move somewhere that doesn't have a pronounced change of seasons. Snow strikes me as one of nature's special wonders that most adults still treasure, before it quickly turns into a slushy brown and gray mess and becomes a major nuisance. And if you have ever been in a major snowstorm—i.e., one that forced the cancellation of everything and actually got adults to slow down for a moment and socialize with unknown neighbors—then you know a bit about the broader magic of snow.

A Small Child's Guide to Wonder

When we were small kids, we had keen senses of wonder and natural inclinations to see magic and possibilities in everything. (See Figure 15.) It wasn't just snowflakes or making snow alligators. We found wonder around every corner and under every rock, where new worlds beyond belief awaited us. Who was to say what was more wonderful given choices including a field full of purple flowers, a gigantic moon glowing in the sky, a plastic box that sang songs, or a bowl of bright red water that would somehow become Jell-O? When we were young, wonder could be found in any new or familiar thing that we had yet to figure out. It could also be found in all the things that seemed amazing to us and stirred our imaginations, or seemed amazing to anyone whose opinion we valued.

Most days we walked around with a permanent Wow! on our faces, ready and willing to be amazed by virtually anything that

Figure 15. A Child's Guide to Wonder

Things That Inspire Wonder

anything new
anything familiar that we can't figure out
anything amazing
anything that someone else thinks is amazing
almost anything in nature (especially animals)
anything that spurs our imaginations

Some Examples:

the man in the moon
bubble bath
dinosaurs
an older sister pretending to be a ghost
eating chocolate for the first time
Jell-O

Things That Do Not Inspire Wonder

anything that is familiar and boring
some things that we have already figured out

came our way and eager to use our imaginations to compound the wonder. Try to remember the last time you spent a day being truly amazed as an adult by most of the things you encountered. If you're lucky and in the right frame of mind, you might have experienced wonder walking through the woods, spending the day at a favorite museum, or taking a vacation in a new and very different place. It certainly doesn't happen very often in the world of business (unless we are part of a team on the verge of a major breakthrough).

> **Won-der**, n. *a marvel; that which arouses astonishment, awe, and a sense of Wow! (i.e., almost everything new or special)*

Wonder is an essential part of a child's ability to learn and grow. It stirs interest, curiosity, and the desire to ask a million questions in order to figure things out. It also provides a wide landscape for unleashing a child's imagination and creativity in a world where anything seems to be possible. If birds, kites, and airplanes can fly, there is no reason to believe that other creatures and objects can't fly as well. If flowers, perfumes, freshly baked cookies, and not exactly "tear-free" shampoos all have pleasing smells, there is no reason to believe that all kinds of other things can't smell beautiful, too. If animals such as purple dinosaurs, big red dogs, and aardvarks dressed in children's clothes can speak, there is no reason to believe that other animals and things can't talk, too. If someone can tickle me, there is no reason why I can't tickle Mom, Dad, a snail, or a book and get the same response.

The existence of so many amazing things to behold and experience suggests to a child that nothing is cut-and-dried. As we get older, we are taught to seek the one right answer, typically an answer that is practical and doable without a lot of extra thinking.

But in a world filled with wonder, we know there are also worlds of possible explanations and understandings, even if they challenge us to stretch our brains. Why should we stop at a snowman, when we can make snowwomen and a cast of other snow characters to delight the senses and the imagination?

Kids see wonder in everything because wonder is in everything. As adults we tend to take most things for granted and bestow the title of wonderful upon a very small subset of the universe. We forget the magic of the big picture and of its smallest details. We don't expect wonder to be around every corner or behind an old barn or at the bottom of a wishing well. For us, wonder disappears when something becomes familiar; as if casually knowing something makes it known to us. To kids, the better they know it, the more wonderful it becomes.

When we were small children, we had no concept of the word *impossible*. As our imaginations grew, we could even conceive of things far beyond the realm of adult possibilities. We imagined worlds in far-off lands and worlds beneath our feet. We looked with amazement at little animals crawling into homes in trees and holes in the ground. We thought of incredible exploits to go on with friends and of incredible new imaginary friends to take on everyday journeys. We imagined ourselves riding beautiful horses or climbing to the tops of great pyramids. We wondered what it would be like to fly like a bird, be as majestic as a butterfly, or run as fast as the wind. In our mind's eye we saw no limits to what we could do, and our imagination and wonder helped frame our keen ability to learn. As kids we truly believed we could learn anything—like a new language, how to add and subtract, or how to play the guitar—in no time at all. When told that things were not possible, we often begged to differ and gladly tried to prove otherwise.

The Challenge for Companies and Their Leaders

Winning in business is all about having bold dreams and using enthusiasm, skill, and perseverance to make them come true. In today's business world, more than ever before, it is important to have a sense of wonder. After all, so many competitors have so many new offerings and ideas about how to do business. And so much of the conventional thinking about products, services, distribution, where and how we work, etc., is being called into question. So if we don't cast our nets for the big ideas across all areas of our businesses, we are likely to be out of the game more quickly than we ever imagined.

Unfortunately, most companies focus their attentions on incremental thinking, incremental change, and incremental improvements in their short-term performances. This occurs even though we know that in today's business world we cannot win with 10 percent more revenue this year, 20 percent more profit next year, and three new products to be launched if we are lucky. We need to shake things up and imagine new worlds and perfect snowflakes. The most successful companies regularly rethink their entire businesses and those things that give them competitive advantage. They don't always change their industries or products and services; but they do seek to determine what the cutting edge can and should be in their industries and what products and services will take them there before their competitors.

Often a change in technology or the application of new technology in a new or different way is required. Tapping and applying technology, in particular information technology, is one of the most obvious ways in which a willingness to wonder can transform almost any business.

A good example is Buckman Laboratories, a leading manufacturer of specialty chemicals that found itself stuck in a commodity business with shrinking margins and a growing number of worldwide competitors. The company imagined what would happen if it used the power of information technology to change its relationship with employees and customers. By developing a robust intranet that allowed the company's workforce to communicate in real time, share their knowledge worldwide, and quickly find the best solutions for any customer at any time, it added unique value and gained a clear edge in its market. But technology isn't the only key driver of change. The guiding principle of wonder is that anything is possible if we are open to seeing it or have the imagination to dream it.

Wonder also enables us to look beyond simply incremental change to quantum leaps in how we think and what we offer to the marketplace. It inspired companies like Ciba Animal Health (now a division of Novartis) to imagine a world where dogs and cats no longer had fleas, rather than a world where we improve the performance of our flea-treating insecticides. It inspired Saab to imagine a car that actually cleans the air while running, rather than a world where we try to reduce the emissions we generate. It inspires us to think of software and human genes that actually fix themselves when they break down, or that can be repaired through the Internet from a small town in Iowa, rather than relying on a technician who might arrive between the hours of 8:00 A.M. and 5:00 P.M. next Wednesday. It also inspires us to think about what it would take to guarantee our products and services forever, rather than simply provide a limited warranty that lasts ninety days longer than our competitors'. Wonder even inspires us to look to the world of nature for new ways to design our products.

Encouraging wonder should also include challenging all of our people to use their imaginations and think in different ways. It means asking people to look at the world around them for new ideas and inspiration that can be translated into real improvements in the way we do business. Wonder is really an attitude about the world. If we believe that magic waits around every corner and we are open to it, we will begin to look for it in everything we do, not just in the industry publications or market studies that land on our desks.

Let's go back to what inspired wonder in us as small children, so we can rediscover what can and should inspire us as grown-ups at work. Remember we marveled at things that were

- new
- difficult to figure out
- cool to us
- cool to someone whose opinion we valued
- found in nature

Now let's relate these to the world of our businesses, and commit to seeing wonder in new images of our industries or marketplaces and to all the things we do that are cool but could be even cooler.

Unfortunately, most companies are neither skilled nor comfortable with having their people think about brave new ways to do business. They have set ways of thinking and set expectations for how to do things. But imagine how much more successful your company would be if most of your people were truly inspired to see the possibilities for wonder in your business and in the customers you served. (See Figure 16.) What if your people cast a wide net for new ideas and best practices across all industries and disciplines? What if your people were eager not only to build snow alligators for your customers but also to help them see the magic in snow alligators?

To get a quick handle on what is possible, look at the wonder being spawned by the Internet and how it is changing the business practices of companies in all industries. Then think about the wonder possible in the convergence of all the media we currently use, including computers, telecommunications, cable TV, and the Internet. Think about what is possible when we unravel the genetic makeup of human beings in order to improve the quality of their health and lives. Using this analogy, try to think about how you might unravel the genetic codes of your customers and their businesses. What would you discover, and how would you put that learning to work to improve the quality of their health and long-term viability? How would you change the way you do business and the nature of your offerings if anything was possible?

Big Lesson #6

We can only reach our full potential when we start to see a world filled with wonder and possibilities.

Figure 16. A Corporate Guide to Wonder

Things That Should Inspire a Sense of Wonder

the needs of our customers and partners
our vision and strategy
our products and services
whatever makes us special as a company
ways to enable our employees to excel
new ideas
important problems and opportunities
the possibilities of technology
insight and best practices from other industries and disciplines

Things That Should Not Inspire a Sense of Wonder

anything that is not important
yesterday's news
anything that does not help us to achieve our vision and
    strategy
anything that cannot strengthen our competitive position

Summary

For a small child, wonder and imagination provide the basis for learning and growing. Kids innately understand that magic is in everything and the world offers more opportunities to those open to seeing all of its possibilities. As adults in companies, we should see the compelling logic of making alligators in the snow, finding new solutions to our customers' pressing problems, or reinventing the rules for our industries.

> *A child's world is fresh and new and beautiful, full of wonder and excitement. It is our misfortune that for most of us that clear-eyed vision, that true instinct for what is beautiful and awe-inspiring, is dimmed and even lost before we reach adulthood.*
>
> RACHEL CARSON

Lessons from the Sandbox

Wonder

- We can only reach our full potential when we start to see a world filled with wonder and possibilities.

- Wonder can be found in everything— from the big picture to the smallest details.

- If you can imagine something, you can make it happen.

- Be open to the unexpected.

- Never forget you can make more out of snow than a man with a carrot nose.

Just for Fun *and* Profit

Here are some things you can do today to rediscover the gift of wonder in order to improve your company's or business unit's bottom-line success.

Check Your Wonder Quotient

When was the last time you actually wondered about a world filled with possibilities? To get started again, make a list of all the important things on your plate that could benefit from wonder. Then pick one to explore and ask some big questions about what is possible if there were no constraints on your imagination, budget, or practicality. You can work out the details later.

Act Your Shoe Size

Spend at least fifteen minutes a day acting (i.e., wondering) like a small child. Your shoe size is probably too large, but you get the idea. Pretend you are two, three, or four years old and take a walk around the office or attend a meeting with your eyes wide open in search of wonder. Make a list of all the things you uncover that are filled with potential for wonder. Then narrow in on the ones that could truly broaden your business potential given the focus of your company. Share your ideas with colleagues.

Visit a Museum

Spend a day at a museum of your choice getting ideas for improving an area of your business. Pick an art museum, science museum, children's museum, or museum of natural history. Find things in the museum that cause you to wonder about and imagine possibilities that could improve your business performance.

7

The Gift of Curiosity

To compete successfully in the future, companies will need to look at themselves and their world with greater curiosity.

Companies spend lots of time and money trying to improve their performance through a wide range of initiatives aimed at quality, productivity, reengineering, customer service, and the like. But they rarely challenge their people to be consistently curious about the business, the marketplace, and the world around them as the basis for making big and small breakthroughs.

Small children constantly try to figure out how things work and how to make them better. The ways they probe and test things and processes to gain a clearer understanding offer radically simple guidance to companies in pursuit of excellence.

It's the little things that make the big things possible. Only close attention to the fine details of any operation makes the operation first-class.

J. WILLARD MARRIOTT, FOUNDER,
MARRIOTT

Today George was curious about the big box on the man's desk.

What could be in it? George could not resist. He simply HAD to open it.

It was full of funny little pieces of all sorts of shapes and all sorts of colors.

George took one out. It looked like a piece of candy.

Maybe it WAS candy. Maybe he could eat it. George put the piece in his mouth—and before he knew, he had swallowed it.

MARGRET AND H. A. REY, *CURIOUS GEORGE GOES TO THE HOSPITAL*, 1966

When we were small children, we loved to go to new places where we could explore and discover new things. For many of us a favorite place was the beach or a lake, spots where we could find all different types of creatures and countless things to mess with. Just the mention of going there would make us jump to attention and get "organized" in a hurry. And we would often bring pails and shovels to help in our discoveries. These were the perfect tools for digging up sand, building castles (or at least piles of wet sand), uncovering shells, making giant holes, finding little animals, or pouring water on suspecting family members. Only when we got a bit older would we actually pour water on unsuspecting family members.

"I Know You're in There!"

It isn't hard to imagine what the snail went through when the giant hand of a two-year-old plucked him (or her) off one of the big rocks by the beach and headed off for a cozy spot. "This looks like curtains for me," he probably said, or at least felt, wondering why after all these years of hiding in his shell and avoiding sea-gulls he was now chosen to be the only mollusk in the Atlantic Ocean captured by a small child.

"Hi!" said the small voice, once she had gotten herself comfortable. "Snail?" "Hello!" "Are you there?" followed by a few moments of silence. "I said hi!" she continued. "I know you're in there. Come out and see me." But the snail would not budge. He was, no doubt, hoping for all the world that this was only a dream and that he would wake up safe and sound on his or any other quiet rock far from the prospect of a human, let alone a small human. But the girl was patient and clearly fascinated by his unwillingness to show his face.

Moments passed and as she continued to stare at the snail, the girl began to giggle. "Little snail, cutie pie, come out. Say hi to me!" Then she began to stroke his back (i.e., his shell) figuring a gentle back massage would relax him just as it relaxed her and her sister. "That feels nice?" she asked, wanting desperately to get a response and to eventually bond. She went on for about five minutes, pausing regularly to turn him over to see if he showed any signs of coming out.

Then, with a very soft touch, the girl placed her finger on the bottom of the snail—the soft, wet, and gushy part—and rubbed him some more. "Tickle you!" she said with a big smile. "I can tickle you." After a few more moments of waiting, the snail gave in and cautiously poked his head out to find out what he was up against. Upon finding the girl smiling intently at him, he began to plan his next move. "Hi!" said the girl. "I knew you were in there." But the snail was silent. "It's OK little cutie!" she added. "Will you play with me?" With that, the snail began to stretch his body as if to communicate back that a game with a small child was probably preferable to ending up on the menu of a French restaurant. "What's your name?" the girl asked. "*Gastropoda*," replied the snail, not realizing the girl did not speak Latin. But it didn't matter. They had begun to learn about each other and build a relationship, albeit a temporary one. "What are these things?" she wondered, pointing to his protruding eyes. "They are my eyes, antennae, and basic all-purpose appendages," he answered. "That's funny," said the girl, giggling again but no doubt impressed with the clever design.

A few moments later, it was time to go and the little girl carried the snail back to the rock where she found him. "I will see you tomorrow," she said with a giant smile. "I'd like that," said the snail, or so it must have seemed. Curiosity had conquered the snail.

A Small Child's Guide to Curiosity

When we were small children, we were natural explorers with keen curiosity about everything around us. (See Figure 17.) To us the whole world, down to its minutest details, was a source of great interest, inspiration, and possibilities. We found countless things to uncover, take apart, figure out, and try to put back together before we moved on to the next discovery. It didn't matter if we were at the beach, waiting in a doctor's office, or rolling around on the floor with the dog. Each locale presented more than enough stuff to be curious about, and we welcomed opportunities to make a mess and learn a lot.

> **Cu-ri-os-i-ty**, n. *a desire to know or learn, especially about something new or strange*

Curiosity is an essential part of a small child's ability to learn and grow. Using all of their senses with skill and flair, kids can turn any place into a playground of new learning. While children use all of their senses to learn, they place special emphasis on their sense of touch. It is just too hard for a child to see something and not want to pick it up. When we were kids, touching was an integral

---

Figure 17. A Child's Guide to Curiosity

Things That Small Children Are Curious About

anything new
anything familiar that they can't figure out
anything amazing
anything that someone else thinks is amazing or that
    someone else is playing with
almost anything in nature (especially animals)
anything that spurs the imagination

Some Examples:

- the man in the moon
- bubble bath
- dinosaurs
- an older sister pretending to be a ghost
- a hula hoop
- eating chocolate for the first time
- any creature that lives in a shell
- Jell-O

Things That Small Children Are Not Curious About

anything that is familiar and boring
some things that they have already figured out

---

part of looking. Whenever we spotted anything of interest, we would immediately say, "I look!" or "I see!" as we reached out to touch it.

By contrast, when most adults discover something new, they are content to just take a look, and maybe a quick smell if the item in question is a flower. Small children need to take the flower apart and rub its colors all over their arms and faces. And when they learn about the basics of facial anatomy, they are not content to just look at someone's ears, eyes, nose, and mouth. They have to experience them—playing with ears, poking at eyes, putting fingers in mouths to see what it feels like, and even picking other people's noses. Why not? It's very interesting stuff that cannot really be understood from a book, a mere glance, or an adult's explanation. As adults, we make visual inspections and that is enough for us. We have no great desire to know what's inside a colleague's nose. But while a nose might be an extreme example, we should want to know what is inside a lot of things, how things work, and how they could be made even better.

As kids we didn't stop at simply probing. We quickly learned the importance of studying and testing the things around us. "What are the properties of this thing that I should know about?" was a common refrain. As babies we put everything in our mouths, our bacteria-filled microscope for examining anything found or given to us. As we grew a bit older, we put things through even more paces, stretching them, pulling them apart, throwing them, dropping them, standing on them, putting them in something wet, and writing on them with a permanent marker. If it was a live object like a dog, a cat, or a bug, we remained focused on its every move and behavior for an extended period of time.

Our curiosity also caused us to explore almost everything no matter how disgusting it was. "What's this?" was commonly our question as we roamed familiar and unfamiliar terrain looking for things to get into. But finding things isn't enough for a small child. Kids need to understand what things are and why. They enter into each exploration without any preconceived notions. Why else would they pick up and play with worms, bugs, and the like? When was the last time that as an adult you played with a big slimy worm? It has probably been a while, unless you are an ento-mologist, a gardener, or someone on an unusually high protein diet. Kids act as though they are desperate to know new stuff and unable to dampen their curiosities. It's their nature—anything that looks settled needs to be unsettled.

When was the last time you heard an adult suggest picking up a snail, holding a bee with bare hands, examining a tree branch filled with bugs, pulling a flower apart, jumping in some mud, or dropping something made of glass just to see what happens? Why not do these things? Is it because they are yucky to touch, they are boring, we know enough about them already, we know better, or we just aren't interested? If we only knew that this important practice helps our businesses grow.

The Challenge for Companies and Their Leaders

As you might expect, curiosity is essential for keeping companies at least one step ahead. Unfortunately, most adults and compa-nies have lost their natural desires to explore and be curious. We begin to lose it when we enter school, where the process of turn-ing us into fine upstanding members of society begins in earnest. But to do this, we have to get comfortable with sitting quietly at our desks, waiting our turns, raising our hands to be called on, walking in a straight line to the cafeteria or out to the playground, and coloring inside the lines.

By the time we go to work in companies or other organizations, most of our innate inquisitiveness has been socialized right out of us. Not only that, but most companies then work very hard to reinforce their own set of very specific guidelines for acceptable behavior. I remember being told recently by the managing partner of a leading professional services firm that it was very hard to get his people to come up with new ideas. "After six months of in-depth training in how we do our work here, we pretty much suck the remaining creativity right out of people." He mentioned this with particular frustration, given the fact that his firm is able to recruit many of the brightest people coming out of business schools.

In companies we are taught to be cautious and to do assignments as they are intended to be done. Curiosity is not typically part of the equation. Wandering around in order to explore things is rarely encouraged. We sit in offices or cubicles, do the assigned jobs to the best of our abilities, follow procedures, and take the behaviors we learned in school to higher levels of sophistication. As managers and leaders we often find it too difficult to encourage curiosity, because we are so focused on meeting our short-term objectives. Responding to new things that might challenge what we are trying to do is seen as a potential obstacle. Unlike small kids, we can only take in so much new information!

How unfortunate, when so many of the clues to growing and strengthening our businesses are all around us waiting to be uncovered. They are in our own labs and halls, at our customers' places of business, in the best practices of companies in similar and different industries, in nature and museums, and even in books, magazines, and movies. But we need to be curious enough to look for them, find them, and study them. And we have to be open to the fact that we *can* explore and learn and stretch.

A few years ago a team of senior executives at Rubbermaid were meeting in London. When they were done they decided to visit the British Museum, which houses one of the world's great collections of antiquities and culture. Their assignment was simple—look closely at how people lived in other civilizations and eras with an eye toward the types of activities that Rubbermaid products are intended to serve. Not only was this act of curiosity stimulating, it resulted in several new or improved products.

Curiosity makes us continuously look at things in order to improve them. It asks us to take things apart, put them back together, change how they work, change what they do, and think of new ways to do old things. Do I need this? Should I add that? What if I combined these two things? Curiosity also causes us to look at problems or simple nuisances as real opportunities to discover new ideas.

Curiosity makes us see things around us that could change our abilities to succeed. They could be brilliant ideas from great minds throughout history, best practices from other industries, or even things and events in nature that could lead to a breakthrough. Curiosity led Georges de Mestral during a hike in the Alps in the 1940s to look at how a simple burr attached itself to the leg of a person or the back of a dog. His closer study revealed the underlying property of Velcro. Curiosity led Douglas Engelbart to wonder if people could really interact with computers in an efficient way. His tinkering led to the development of the first graphical user interface—i.e., the computer mouse.

As adults in business, we should be curious about a lot, just as kids are curious about everything that crosses their paths. We should be curious about what our customers need and how their needs are changing; how a world of amazing new technologies can be applied to improve the performances of our products and services and our ability to deliver them; what the new workforce wants from employers; and what will enthuse and energize people to spend most of their waking hours in our organizations. (See Figure 18.)

We need to commit to wandering around, smelling the flowers, and picking up the snails on our way. We need to commit to trying to figure out how things work and how we can make them better. And we need to inspire our people to be curious about those things that could make them more effective in their jobs. If we are responsible for customer service, then we should be curious about the world's best practitioners and should commit to learning what they do, dissecting it, and adapting what we learn in order to improve our operations. If we are responsible for human resources, we should be curious about learning the state-of-the-art in finding, retaining, and motivating great employees. If we are responsible for coming up with new ideas for products and services, we should be very curious about how the leading companies do it, and learn from their experiences even if they are in completely different industries. We should commit to approaching these issues in much the same way as small children begin to understand and relate to snails.

We should be curious about and open to all different types of information that might shed some light on what we are trying to do. Instead, companies tend to subscribe to all the publications and attend all the conferences and trade shows in their industries

---

Figure 18. A Corporate Guide to Curiosity

Things That Most Adults Are Often Curious About

traffic
the weather
how long the line is at the bank
promotion opportunities
the new boss
the consultants who have just appeared
the latest gossip
getting a pay raise

Things That Adults Should Be Curious About

how to do new things
how to do familiar things better
what customers need
how to find and keep great employees
what your competitors are up to
new technologies that could improve your performance
best practices in every industry
a world of ideas and possibilities

---

as though they are the source of everything worth knowing in order to grow the business. Kids grow by being open to and curious about all different kinds of information.

We also need to be open to new people. The freshest time to tap their ideas, perspectives, and brainpowers is when they first arrive in our organizations. That is, before we teach them to act and think like us and follow the constraints we have established to help our organizations grow.

Big Lesson #7

We can only reach our full potential when we start to scratch beneath the surface of things worth understanding.

Summary

In a child's world curiosity is a key to great new insights and sheer delight. Kids know that there are always important secrets to be discovered at quiet beaches, great museums, or teaming marketplaces. As adults in companies we must rediscover the simple fact that curiosity with a purpose in mind is its own reward.

Even when freshly washed and relieved of all obvious confections, children tend to be sticky.

FRAN LEBOWITZ

Lessons from the Sandbox

Curiosity

- We can only reach our full potential when we start to scratch beneath the surface of things worth understanding.

- Use all of your senses to figure things out.

- Never pass up the chance to wander around aimlessly.

- Make sure to learn from new people who have different ways of doing things.

- Make time to befriend snails and other creatures to learn their mysteries (and practice your communication skills).

Just for Fun *and* Profit

Here are some things you can do today to rediscover the gift of curiosity in order to improve your company's or business unit's bottom-line success.

Take a Walk in the Woods

Spend an afternoon walking through the woods to find clues to your company's success. Pick a difficult problem or a new business opportunity that you are wrestling with and see how many ideas you can find for addressing it. What would the natural world and its other inhabitants think about your issue? You'll be surprised at how this bit of curiosity might help. This can be done on your own or as a team; just pick different places to explore.

Become a Kid in a Candy Store

Visit a great candy store and wander around with the curiosity of a small child. Grab a bag and a scooper and pick a wide variety of treats, paying attention to their sizes, shapes, colors, textures, smells, and how you think they might taste. To really get the experience, do this down on your knees so you get a real kid's eye view. You can explore your selections further back at the office with colleagues.

Look at the Details of Something Familiar

Now look at your own product, service, or issue with a child's curiosity. What sticks out? What opportunities exist for coming up with a better result? To the untrained observer, what is too amazing to be true about your current practices?

8

The Gift of Questioning

To COMPETE SUCCESSFULLY in the future, companies will need to ask the right questions and answer them in ways that thrill their customers, employees, and shareholders.

I n our information-based economy, many experts view the ability to learn quickly and continuously as the greatest competitive weapon. But how do we teach adults and companies to learn at the speed of light?

Small children are the definition of nonstop learning in large part because they ask millions of obvious and amazing questions and never take no for an answer. They teach us that learning is not an assignment but a way of life.

Asking the right questions takes as much skill as giving the right answers.

ROBERT HALF, FOUNDER,
ROBERT HALF ASSOCIATES

Do your ears hang low?
Do they wobble to and fro?
Can you tie them in a knot?
Can you tie them in a bow?
Can you throw them o'er your shoulder
Like a continental soldier?
Do your ears hang low?

Do your ears hang high?
Do they reach up to the sky?
Do they wrinkle when they're wet?
Do they straighten when they're dry?
Can you wave them at your neighbor
With an element of flavor?
Do your ears hang high?

CHILDREN'S SONG

Have you ever tried to imagine what it must have been like to live at a time in history when people did not know very much about many things we take for granted today? Not that people were stupid back then, or anything like that—in fact, they were probably very clever. They just didn't have the benefit of our learning, insight, books and magazines, scientific discoveries, or innovations in commerce and household appliances. They certainly didn't have cable TV with all its amazing channels to fall back on. But that didn't stop small children from asking a lot of great questions.

What Are Clouds Made Of?

It wasn't until I became the parent of a small child that I understood why adults in ancient times actually explained things the way they did. Sure the earth was flat as a pancake. Why else would ships and camels disappear over the edge? Of course the winds were the work of the gods. Who else could let off that much steam? Certainly there was a great planet of darkness in the heavens that cast a giant shadow on the earth each night. How else would we know that it was time for kids to go to sleep, so that Mom and Dad could have a few minutes of "alone time" before the roosters welcomed the new day? All perfectly reasonable explanations when faced with a constant barrage of questions from small children.

In ancient times the natural world was filled with much more mystery than it is today. How did most things work? How did they get there? What were their ultimate purposes? Would the gods get really mad if you messed with them? Adults had to be really quick on their feet to seem intelligent and worthy of respect. It's not that science and our current state of learning hold a clear advantage for most of us today. But imagine a typical day in ancient Athens, Rome, Egypt, China, or northern New Jersey, for that matter. Sounds a bit intimidating, doesn't it?

In the twenty-first century it is not that much easier to seem intelligent, and a recent walk through the neighborhood made that perfectly clear to me. It was a beautiful fall day, filled with changing leaves and a bright blue sky punctuated by perfect clouds. Just the kind of day that would make a small child look up and ask, "Papa, what are clouds made of?" This is, of course, a perfectly reasonable question. And it was quickly followed by lots of other perfectly reasonable questions:

"How come some clouds make rain and others don't?"

"Why are there clouds anyway?"

"Is there another way to make rain?"

"What is the moon made of?"

"Why is there a moon anyway?"

"Why is there just one moon?"

"Are there jellyfish on the moon?"

"Is there really a man in the moon?"

"Who else lives on the moon?"

"Does God live on the moon?"

"What does the man in the moon do all day?"

"Does the man in the moon have a daughter just like me?"

Now I do find all these questions to be interesting and stimulating. But as you may gather, I have no formal training as a meteorologist (or an astronomer). Quite frankly, I never considered it as a career. If I had only been more astute in college I might have recognized its pluses. After all, how many professions reward people handsomely and put them on TV when they are dead wrong more than half of the time?

I did have a rough idea that clouds were actually visible collections of particles of water or ice suspended in the air waiting to come down as soon as the next family picnic was about to start. I was also willing to believe that there were many moons on lots and lots of planets, and that some of them probably had either real or imaginary inhabitants. As for the man in the moon, I could only hope he had a daughter who kept him on his toes.

A Small Child's Guide to Questioning

When we were small children, we asked a lot of great questions. It was mostly to learn new things. But it was also to get involved in a conversation, to participate in some meaningful way, and to drive people (especially our parents) crazy. "That's enough questions already," was probably a common refrain from your parents after a deluge of inquiries. I can only guess that Socrates was a kid at heart, asking lots of big questions to uncover ultimate truths. But it might have been just a clever tactic to look smart in a world with many major unknowns.

> **Ques-tion-ing,** v. *the act of asking a million questions in order to understand something special and to find what is desirable and possible*

As small kids we knew the essential questions that quickly went to the heart of almost any matter: what and why as in "What is this?" "What are you doing?" "Why does this thing work this way?" or "Why are we doing this in the first place?" These questions enabled us to figure out if something was special and worth doing. If it was, we had plenty of follow-up questions to pose.

We were also very open and honest in our questions. Unlike most adults, we didn't make an effort to censor our thoughts. We just opened our mouths and asked whatever was on our minds. In addition to questions about nature and the various parts and functions of the human body, we were interested in what other people did for work and play, what options we had at any given time, the purpose and details of bad things that happen to people (like broken arms or legs), the activities of God, and where our siblings actually came from. To put this in perspective, here are some other questions I have been asked by our kids and their friends:

"Why do birds fly?"

"What is an eclipse?"

"Who is God?"

"Does God drive a car?"

"Why are there so many mean people in the world?"

"What is so important about geography?"

"Did they have hotels when you were a kid?"

"Who gave you your bald spot?"

"Do you like to go potty?"

"Can cows play soccer?"

"Would a puppy dog ever eat a small child?"

"Why will I get sick if I drink dirty water?"

"If you burp hard enough will it kill you?"

"Is Grandpa really a space alien?"

"What is a meeting?"

"Why would anyone spend a whole day in a meeting?"

"Why do you go to so many meetings?"

"What do parents do for fun?"

Every child has also asked the question: "Why do I have to finish my vegetables?" And every parent whom I know has replied, "Because they are good for you *and* because there are starving children in China." Unfortunately, by the age of four most kids realize the sheer impossibility of actually getting their unfinished vegetables halfway around the world. In fact, it's becoming harder and harder to fool kids, even though parents still try to whenever they have the energy. I remember the following conversation with our older daughter just after her sister was born:

"Papa, how does Mama make milk to nurse the new baby?"

"That's a great question, sweetheart," I responded, followed by a long "pregnant" pause and a question of my own: "Do you know how cows make milk?"

"They eat grass and it turns into milk?"

"Exactly! And, do you know what Mama does while you are in school?"

"She takes care of my baby sister?"

"Exactly. But while your little sister is taking a nap, Mama goes into the backyard and eats some grass."

"Is that really true, Papa?"

"I'm not a hundred percent sure, but I think so."

Not too bad an answer for a guy living in the year 2000.

The Challenge for Companies and Their Leaders

A few years ago Chrysler decided to remake itself by creating a brand-new line of automobiles and trucks that would "change the way vehicles were designed and built." The key to this effort, as they would proudly report, was a commitment to "question everything." The process was certainly not original. After all, kids have been doing just that since the beginning of time. But the result was a dramatic turnaround in their corporate fortunes and bottom-line performance.

Their questioning, we can only assume, was tied to a strong curiosity about what it would take to build a better car. But it raises a more essential point. We can only understand and improve things if we are willing to ask the right questions and answer them in ways that will improve the value we provide to our customers, employees, and other shareholders. To do this, we must challenge everyone in the organization to ask tough questions and be willing to find the best answers and act on them. All in all, it's not a bad idea to regularly question everything.

This doesn't apply just to technology-driven companies, though it is clear that they must constantly question and refine their business models, products, services, and practices. It also applies to every company that sells anything directly to a consumer and is likely to be affected by changes in what people buy and how they prefer to "shop." You can rest assured that the smartest minds at leading firms like Nike, The Gap, and The Sharper Image are up most nights asking questions about the world around them and thinking about how to create or ride the next wave. You can also be sure that most companies are investing lots of time and money questioning the best ways to capitalize on and integrate on-line commerce as a channel for their offerings.

But is this a quantum change in the way that business is done or just another important innovation moving at a faster pace? While we are in the midst of the Internet shopping revolution, it is fun to note that in the 1870s a young man in Chicago decided to question the very basis of retail shopping. His breakthrough idea, the mail-order catalog, is now 125 years old, and still alive and kicking. His name, in case you wonder, was Aaron Montgomery Ward.

Asking questions is essential to doing a better job and growing. As far as we know, no one ever came up with a powerful new idea without questioning the assumption on which old thinking was based or asking an entirely new question. Questions also help us to understand things better. We start by asking *what* and *why* to make sure we know if what we are doing makes sense. We should ask regularly what is going on in our marketplace and the world around it with special emphasis on our customers' needs. In fact, we should be asking our customers questions all the time in order to learn how well we are meeting their needs, what additional needs they have, and what is going on in their world that affects their use of our products and services.

Asking the right questions can also help us to have a common focus and challenge us to work together more effectively to come up with the best answers. Asking questions like: "How do we become the leading provider in our industry?" or "How do we raise the bar in terms of the quality of our offerings?" or "How do we gain a competitive advantage through the use of technology?" gets company employees all on the same page and working toward improving performance. In times of great change we need to ask questions that will help us improve our performances all the time and answer our questions faster and more skillfully and passionately than will our competitors.

But what specific types of questions should we ask? Figure 19 lists some important questions that businesses should ask on a regular basis. Let's say we want to reduce the cost of producing our products or delivering our services in order to gain a significant advantage over our competitors. We could begin by asking some fundamental questions about why we do things the way we do and if there is an entirely better way. We can zoom in on specific areas of our operations to determine where the best payoff from changes or new investments might be. We can also ask a series of "What if?" questions to stretch our thinking about the best possible solutions. In any event, the notion of questioning everything is compelling. Figure 20 identifies the five basic questions to ask in trying to get things done.

Questions can help us to be more creative and to think "out of the box." Let's assume that we want to improve customer service. We could certainly ask a few basic questions to get started: "What are the current concerns our customers have with our service?" or "What are the key issues we face in providing customer service?" or "What are the possible actions we could take to do a better job?" But we could also test our creativity and commitment by asking some tougher questions: "What would we do if we were committed to delivering the highest level of customer service in the world?" or "What would we do if we wanted to

---

Figure 19. Important Business Questions

What business are we in?
Who are our customers?
What is important to them?
What, if anything, sets us apart today?
Why do we do things the way we do?
What if we did things differently?
What should set us apart tomorrow?
How could we reinvent our business?
What is our formula for making a profit?
How do we get the best from our people?
Are we yawst?

---

provide the worst customer service in the world?" The latter question gives us a chance to have some fun before we look at our own warts. By first figuring out the worst possible service, we can then look at its opposite in a new and more challenging light.

Asking the right questions should be part of the very nature of doing business today. So much is changing so fast that we need to collect enough of the right information to frame our decisions and act accordingly. We should use questions to keep us on target with what makes us special so we don't become just one of the pack.

Big Lesson #8

We can only learn and grow if we are willing to ask a lot of good questions.

Figure 20. Getting Things Done

Five Essential Questions	Child's Answer	Adult's Answer
Who?	Me!	You.
What?	Mine!	Whatever.
Where?	Here!	There.
How?	My way!	However.
When?	Now!	Later.

Summary

We win in business today by questioning everything that matters most and answering those questions in ways that delight our customers, employees, and shareholders. It's a simple lesson worth relearning any day there's a cloud in the sky.

> *One hour with a child is like a ten-mile run.*
>
> JOAN BENOIT SAMUELSON

Lessons from the Sandbox

Questioning

- We can only learn and grow if we are willing to ask a lot of good questions.

- Question everything that is important and worth doing.

- Don't accept no for an answer.

- Don't accept yes for an answer.

- Never dismiss a creative answer to a complicated question.

- Don't expect a great answer when asking adults about the weather.

Just for Fun *and* Profit

Here are some things you can do today to rediscover the gift of questioning in order to improve your company's or business unit's bottom-line success.

Ask a Million Questions in an Hour

Start by picking something you are curious about outside of work. It can be a hobby you enjoy, something found in nature, or an idea from an article or book that caught your attention. Make a list of all the questions you could ask to become smarter about what you picked. Go through your list and pick five important questions; answer them with a spirit of curiosity and passion.

Go to Extremes

One great way to continually improve your business is to ask some "extreme" questions in order to stimulate your best thinking. For example: "How would we make perfect products that last forever?" or "How would we create an ideal workplace where people beg to be our employees and no one ever leaves?" We can also ask the flip side of these questions: "How could we make the worst products in history?" or "How could we create a workplace so awful that everyone wants to leave after their first day on the job?" Try extreme questions as a way to gain new insights into something important. You'll be surprised at what such questions stimulate. You can do this with your team members.

Spend a Day Questioning Everything

Practice this gift by coming up with good questions for everything around you.

9

The Gift of Trying

To compete successfully in the future, companies will need to try new things and make faster and more intelligent mistakes.

An essential ingredient in growing a business is the ability to try new things and to take informed and timely risks. But too many companies lose the knack for taking necessary chances as they grow bigger, older, and presumably wiser.

Small children are always testing the limits of their own abilities, their parents' patience, and the physical properties of live creatures and inanimate objects. They show us that the only way to keep growing is by taking educated leaps of skill and faith.

We don't grow unless we take risks.
Any successful company is riddled with
failures.

JAMES E. BURKE, CHAIRMAN,
JOHNSON & JOHNSON

At the top of a very tall tree, Verdi gripped one branch with his tail and another with his little snake jaws. I will never be lazy, boring, or green! he thought. I will jump and climb and keep moving so fast that I will stay yellow and striped forever.

Then Verdi let go . . .

From a distance the greens watched. "Oh, my," they chorused.

Ribbon shook his head. "At this rate, he'll be lucky to make it to his first molt."

Aggie nodded. "He's likely to put an eye out on a branch." Umbels moaned. "He may not live to turn green."

JANELL CANNON, *VERDI*, 1997

When we were small children, playgrounds were much different and more dangerous than they are today. No smooth, safe, and ergonomically designed equipment to protect our little bodies, or tree bark and foam rubber squares to cushion our many falls. No sculpted plastic slides that never got hot enough to burn our hands or legs on sunny summer days. And no rust-free beams and hidden hardware to keep us from getting scraped. When we were kids, we had real playgrounds where everything was made out of very strong steel, where swings and seesaws could launch us into space if our weight wasn't balanced perfectly, and where everything hovered over firm and inviting landing areas made out of the finest asphalt available. In retrospect one could only ask, "What in the world were adults thinking when they designed that stuff?" But it actually didn't matter to us, because we didn't know any better, and because any playground was (and always will be) a perfect place to have fun and try new things.

"Don't Worry, I Can Do It!"

Go to a playground on any nice day and you are likely to see kids of all ages having fun and trying new things, just like when you were young. The big kids are busy seeing how high they can swing, how fast they can climb on parts of the equipment that were not meant for climbing, or how many new ways they can conceive of to break their bones on the slide. Smaller kids are busy trying to master new pieces of equipment or improve their skills on familiar ones, and everyone is burning off lots of energy in the process. If you watch long enough, you will probably see at least one little guy or gal, just turned two-years-old, preparing to stretch the bounds of his or her universe by climbing on the jungle gym or swinging in a big kid's swing. Now imagine you are that small child, and you are standing right under the jungle gym looking up in awe.

"Wow!" you probably say to yourself, in a voice filled with enthusiasm and a slight bit of fear, as you gaze from your thirty-inch-tall vantage point at this veritable skyscraper of steel bars and joints. "This is the coolest thing to climb in all of history!" Today is the day you are determined to try your hand at this important test of childhood. So there you stand, looking up for another moment, knowing that it must be climbed and you have been chosen to make the ascent. Exactly who chose you is unclear, but that doesn't matter. Now it's time to concentrate—for a good five seconds or as long you're able to.

You focus on the first rung and then the second, moving your eyes back and forth to plan your attack. "That's what I need to hold on to," you tell yourself, "and that's where I need to put my feet." Letting go of Mom's hand, you reach up to touch the bar. "It's hot," you tell yourself, not because you are looking for excuses to stop but because you find it helpful to collect as much data as possible when determining what to try and how to do it. "Can I lift you up?" Mom asks. "Self!" you reply. "It's pretty high up. I can help you just a little," she continues. "No! Self!" you insist as you grasp the second rung tightly with one hand. "I do by self!" Cautiously letting go of Mom's hand, you place your other hand on the bar and begin to pull yourself up. You groan for effect and to keep Mom completely focused on your need for backup at any minute. (Little do you know at that time that a well-timed groan will become an important habit to rely on when you enter the world of work.) You place one foot on the lower rung. It feels good.

"I try!" you tell Mom, glancing back once more for reassurance. But Mom looks worried. "Don't worry, I can do it!" you say. You place your other foot on the lower rung. "We have liftoff!" you tell yourself, as you look down to see the ground below. After a big smile, you reach up to grasp the third rung with one hand and then two. You lift one foot onto the second rung and then the other foot. Then you turn to Mom, who is standing three inches behind you looking both proud and fearful, to smile and indicate that you are ready to come down. "Help!" you yell, somehow knowing that even astronauts get rescued upon reentry. "Good job!" Mom replies. "I *almost* did it!" you answer, with a look that says you will complete the job tomorrow, or the next day, or whenever the spirit moves you. That was three rungs today and the final three next time. Then you'll be on top of the world.

A Small Child's Guide to Trying

When we were small children, we spent much of each day trying new things. It wasn't so tough then, because most things were new to us and we had little reason to fear any great consequences of our actions. In fact, we didn't have any clear concept of failure. When we didn't quite succeed, we paused to think about whether or not we should try again. Usually, we got right back at it. Unless, of course, the activity or the result was too painful or scary. If not, we would keep trying until we got it right. After all, falling off the chair was not a good reason to avoid trying to climb on the table. And breaking an arm was a perfect badge of courage for a child eager to master everything the world had to offer. Mountain climbers might say that they climbed a particular peak "because it was there." Kids try almost anything because they are there.

When we were small kids, we quickly determined whether or not something was fun and worth doing. If it was, we kept at it, getting better with each attempt until we finally mastered it. If it wasn't, we quickly moved on to something else. This process of nonstop trying produced amazing results in terms of learning and growth.

We were particularly determined to try anything that other kids were doing, especially older kids. While we were often a bit cautious at first, we quickly dove right in anyhow and learned to say, "I try!" and "Self!" or "Myself!" then eventually "I try myself!" and then once we became a bit older, "Don't help me, I'd rather do it myself!" or "Stand back! I am going to do it all by myself!" Think about the last time you said "I try!" at work. Of course, you are saying "I try" when you accept a new assignment, sign up for training, or give blood. But how often do we really take on totally new and tall mountains to climb?

Try-ing, v. *the act of attempting to do something special in order to understand it and what is desirable and possible*

Sometimes trying was so rewarding that we couldn't stop doing it. Remember the way we learned to put on our own jackets as small kids? We would take the jacket and lay it down on the floor backward. Then we would kneel down, sneak our arms into the sleeves and flip it back over our heads. After getting it stuck on our head a few times, we quickly got the hang of it. Once we did, we were eager to demonstrate this new skill to anyone who would watch, and we even tried it with other people's coats when we saw them lying on the floor.

Often, trying resulted in short-term progress followed by a period of regression. A classic case was learning to use utensils at the dinner table. This took a lot of concentration and coordination until we almost got the hang of it. For a short period of time, it was fun to demonstrate this new skill and receive lots of positive reinforcement. But many of us then quickly regressed to eating the natural way, using our hands to gain a more complete sensory experience. Why not? It worked for the Vikings for several hundred years, as well as for many other civilized barbarians. Finally, at the age of six or seven, we succeeded in dining in the most socially acceptable way that the Western world has to offer. Watching a small child struggle to use his or her spoon, fork, and knife will give you greater appreciation for kids' dexterity in countries that use chopsticks.

Trying comes so naturally to small children. I recall being at a paint store to have a special color mixed when a one-year-old wandered over to the mixing machine as it was shaking away. Without any hesitation she began to shake her entire body up and down and side to side just like the machine. This looked like too much fun to not try it!

The Challenge for Companies and Their Leaders

Several years ago I met with the leadership team of a large telecommunications corporation to talk about the keys to innovation and developing better new products. After much discussion, the CEO acknowledged that the company had no shortage of good ideas. What they lacked was skill in picking the best ones, trying them out, and learning quickly from their mistakes. "We are not very good at failing and growing from the experience," he admitted with great frustration. "I guess you could say that we have an uncommon propensity for repetitive error."

I always recall his comments when thinking about trying as a critical step in business success and creating magic. Unfortunately, too many companies lose the knack for trying to do new things and the knack for learning from the up-front work involved in mastering any new skill. Over time, many of the same companies simply stop trying.

For kids, adults, and companies, trying new things can be scary because it takes us out of our comfort zones. But unlike small kids, adults are conditioned to believe that failure is always a real option. And failure has a cost, even if it is just a loss of confidence or self-esteem. No matter what you read in the popular business press, very few companies actually reward their people for screwing up—especially when they screw up big-time. So we have to be pretty sure we are going to succeed, before we decide to take on anything new. That typically means trying new things that are only incrementally different from the things we have done before.

Most successful companies have had their share of significant failures. After all, it is hard to be perfect 100 percent of the time. Sometimes these mistakes actually make it to market, as in the case of the Edsel and New Coke, and sometimes they never see the light of day. Other times companies launch products that still have bugs to work out in order to get them to market as quickly as possible. This is a common practice in the world of software where time is of the essence and improvements in the form of upgrades are intended to correct small and large mistakes without derailing a new product.

Many companies have even turned "mistakes" into very successful products and services. 3M's Scotchgard fabric protector is a good example. In the 1950s, a team of researchers was working with fluorochemicals that could be used on airplanes. When one of the team members inadvertently spilled one of the chemicals on her tennis shoe, she noticed that it was practically impossible to get off. And over time it was even harder to stain. Or look at Upjohn's Rogaine, a widely sold treatment for hair loss. This product was originally intended as a treatment for ulcers. But researchers working with it noticed that while the laboratory rats were still sick to their stomachs, they had quickly become the hairiest rodents on the face of the earth. If only it was so easy to grow hair on the head of a man.

As companies, we need to encourage all of our people to try new things on a regular basis, recognizing that the act of trying is vital to our long-term growth and success. We also need to acknowledge that it is OK to make mistakes along the way as long as we learn from them and get closer to doing it right. We can reward people for making the effort to do something worthwhile as much as we reward them for being successful. Otherwise, we cannot expect them to step out of their comfort zones when we really need them to stretch. We need to stand behind them to offer a helping hand, knowing that in time they will have less need for a safety net. As organizations, we need to learn to quickly capture the insight gained from trying and incorporate it into our continuing effort to improve the next time.

There are also issues to deal with if we are successful in trying something new. The biggest one is getting other people to go along and adopt our ideas, or at least learn the lessons that come from them. Let's assume that we figure out a new way to manufacture our product, support our customers, or collect essential data. We would then need to change the way we do things. But change means disrupting the status quo, and people will quickly step up to question whether the change is worth the investment. They will be armed with plenty of ammunition from all of the other changes we made that did not deliver the intended results and cost a ton of money.

But we can't win in business until we are willing to try new and bold things. We also need to try them faster and faster and improve our skills in learning from any missteps we make along the way. The issue isn't whether we screw up, but how quickly we get it right and how persistent we are in mastering those things worth doing and making them part of the life of our organizations.

Obviously, we don't want to try everything in business, but we want to be open to trying things that make sense given our focus and strategy. We also want to be very serious and passionate about the things we do try. Too many companies fail to really try when they fail to commit the resources required to do something well, including not only money, but people, energy, and commitment. We also need a process for trying (with clear criteria to guide what we try and clear metrics to help us gauge the value and our progress).

Most important, we need to view learning new things as part of the everyday nature of life, work, and growth.

Big Lesson #9

We can only learn and grow if we are willing to try new things.

Summary

In a small child's world, learning new things comes quite naturally and with only a little hesitation. Trying is the name we give to every first step on the road to figuring out something worth doing. Success is the name we give to our best efforts and the learning that comes with them. Together, we can set our next challenge when we get to the monkey bars.

> *The child is a natural investigator—testing, fumbling, and endlessly repeating.*
>
> MARGARET MCINTYRE

Lessons from the Sandbox

Trying

- We can only learn and grow if we are willing to try new things.

- Trying to do something worth doing is its own reward.

- To err is human, and possibly divine . . . as long as we learn from our mistakes.

- It is better to try something than to curse the darkness.

- The right encouragement is often better than having a lot of talent.

- Make sure that you have adult supervision the first time you try something dangerous.

Just for Fun *and* Profit

Here are some things you can do today to rediscover the gift of trying in order to improve your company's or business unit's bottom-line success.

Gauge Your Willingness to Try

Spend fifteen minutes to make an honest assessment of your willingness to try new things at work and in your personal life. Start by making a list of all the new things you have tried in the past year and the benefits of doing them. Note the ones that came naturally and the ones that were fraught with even the slightest bit of anxiety. What caused your blood pressure to go up? Think about the results of your efforts and how you might improve your comfort level about trying new things that are difficult but worth doing.

Pick a New Skill to Master

Think of a new skill you have been wanting to learn but have never found the time to work on. Then put together a quick game plan for making it happen. It can be something artistic or creative, like learning to paint or playing the harmonica, or something very practical like baking a perfect bread or building a cabinet. But get started today and prove to yourself that trying something new is its own reward.

Ask a Small Child for Help

Ask a small child what it is like for him or her to try something new and how he or she deals with fear. The results will surprise and encourage you.

10

The Gift of Creativity
and Innovation

To compete successfully in the future, companies will
need to innovate consistently and skillfully in all aspects
of their businesses.

I nnovation is the lifeblood of companies. To survive and prosper, companies must consistently create successful new products, services, and new ways of doing business. But how do
we dramatically increase the level of creativity and profitable
innovation?

The everyday life of a small child is an endless parade of new
ideas and invention. Children are natural innovators and builders
who find inspiration in a quiet pond, a bird in flight, a ball, a
snowflake, a package of cake mix, or their father's thinning hair.
They teach us that new ideas and business opportunities are
everywhere if we only have the willingness to make the right
connections.

> *Creativity is the sudden cessation of stupidity.*
>
> EDWIN LAND, FOUNDER, POLAROID

I've done it, I've done it!

Guess what I've done!

Invented a light that plugs into the sun.

The sun is bright enough,

The bulb is strong enough,

But, oh, there's only one thing wrong . . .

The cord ain't long enough.

SHEL SILVERSTEIN, "INVENTION,"
WHERE THE SIDEWALK ENDS, 1974

Throughout modern history, the kitchen has been the scene of some of the world's great experiments and inventions. Innovators and would-be innovators, lacking the resources to create suitable workshops, quite naturally found kitchens to their liking. After all, kitchens were places with counter space, access to water, lots of containers for mixing liquids and solids, a floor that could be mopped up, ready access to a range of stylish aprons, and an easy escape route should something go wrong. It is said by less than reliable sources that Edison initially conceived of the lightbulb in the kitchen and that the Wright Brothers' first sketches of their airplane were stained all over with ketchup and mustard. The most amazing moments of sheer creativity in a kitchen, however, have probably been when small kids were involved.

"Try It, You'll Love It!"

Imagine yourself as a small child stuck in the house on a rainy afternoon. Mom has come up with a brilliant scheme to keep you from watching TV and destroying some of your finest brain cells. "Let's bake something in the kitchen," Mom suggests, knowing this is an assignment no self-respecting child can pass up. Needing no further arm-twisting or bribery, you sprint into the kitchen with an eye toward making something very special; though like many great inventors of the past, you have no idea what the final product will actually be.

First you need to help Mom bake banana bread. Actually, it is not a bad way to apprentice on your way to learning enough to warrant your own laboratory, equipment, and budget. It turns out to be plenty of fun, if for no other reason than that it includes smushing old bananas, mixing them with other good stuff, getting to hold Mom's hand while she guides the mixer through its paces, pouring the gloppy batter into a greased bread pan, and licking the spatula and the bowl. Nice job, if you can get it.

Now that the banana bread is in the oven, it's your turn to work some magic. You mobilize all of the equipment you will need for your creation—e.g., plenty of mixing bowls, wooden spoons, measuring cups, a pitcher for water, and a host of dry, wet, and semiarid ingredients. You pile as much of this stuff on the counter as possible, realizing you can never have too many ingredients when concocting something new. Now it's time to begin your search for the ultimate truths of science, chaos, and mess making.

Initially, at least, you receive a fair amount of parental encouragement. After all, one person's catastrophe is another person's winning entry in the Pillsbury Bake-Off. Besides, your Mom has made sure that none of the items available can be combined to create something explosive. Her fantasy, of course, is that you will someday cook dinner for the whole family, relieving her of the burden of creating one more pasta recipe that everyone will tolerate.

The first step is to test the concept of liquid volume. To do this, you take a small measuring cup and fill it with water. Then you empty its contents into a large pitcher. You repeat this step several times until you have filled the large pitcher to the top. For some reason known only to a small child and possibly a few of the most creative thinkers at the National Institute for Water Science, you decide to reverse the process and empty the contents of the large pitcher into the measuring cup. This experiment yields a full measuring cup and sends the remaining 56 ounces of water (or roughly 1.57 liters) all over the counter, floor, and your clothes. Turning to Mom you say, "Look, I spilled!" leaving her to assume that the first part of your work has been a great success far exceeding any of your expectations.

Now it's time to actually make something. You take a large bowl and begin to squeeze as much ketchup into it as possible; then you add some fresh red peppers, a tomato, some flour, some powdered sugar, a few shakes of cinnamon, a swig of maple syrup, and a slice of premium-quality American cheese. "We have to mix it very carefully," you explain. "But what are you making?" Mom asks, not exactly eager to taste this bright red concoction. "I'm making salsa in a cup!" After the mixing is done, you give it a taste. "That's spicy!" you note. "I think it needs some chocolate syrup." You add the last ingredient with a look of pride and great accomplishment. "Ready to try?" you ask Mom, as the dog proceeds to hide under the table. "Sure," she replies, checking to make sure that the phone number for the poison hot line is close at hand.

"Not bad at all."—the exact same words uttered by Alexander Graham Bell upon making his first phone call.

A Small Child's Guide to Creativity

When we were small children, we were masters of creativity and innovation, making new connections and throwing everything into a mixing bowl at practically every turn. We had some great advantages over adults, which helped us come up with new ideas. These advantages included the right degree of ignorance and a willingness to put the most unlikely things together just for the fun (and curiosity) of it. They also included, as we saw in the last chapter, an openness to trying new things and a predisposition for action. While adults might ponder the merits of something for an inordinate amount of time, kids just try it. Whoever came up with the "Just Do It!" slogan for Nike must have hung out with small children.

The power of ignorance runs counter to our notion of how new ideas and breakthroughs actually occur. While small kids are learning incredible amounts of new stuff all the time, they do not hold hard-and-fast notions about people, animals, inanimate objects, and the purposes and properties of everything around them. As a result, unfamiliar things can truly be anything and even familiar things are filled with possibilities. Kids don't look at certain things and assume that they can serve only single purposes. Knowing too much about something often limits our ability to creatively think about it and capitalize on its attributes in new and interesting ways. So while kids ask "Why?" a lot of times, they ask "Why not?" just as often. Why not put chocolate syrup in lemonade? Why not put training wheels on a horse so you won't tip over if you ride too fast? Why not combine a scissors with a comb so you can keep your hair trimmed all the time? Why not create a health club for dolls and stuffed animals so they can get exercise and stay in shape, too? Why not make food-resistant clothing? Why not put caffeine in birdseed so birds can sing in the nighttime too? Hearing birds sing would make it much easier for kids to fall asleep.

In-no-vat-ing, v. *the act of coming up with something new and of real value*

These questions and the innovations they spark are directly due to a child's ability to make very logical connections between things that don't go together in an adult's mind. From a kid's perspective, however, everything can possibly go with everything else. In fact, the whole world is up for grabs. Besides, making the same connections as everyone else is downright boring. So spend a few minutes seriously thinking about the innovations in Figure 21 and the thought processes that led to them. Just so you know, they were all created by small kids in my neighborhood. Then try to apply this way of looking at the world to your company and what it offers.

In addition to being open-minded, small kids rarely think that anything is a bad idea. On the contrary, everything has the potential to be cool. You rarely ever hear a small child say, "That is the dumbest idea I ever heard!" or "Are you out of your mind!" or "What were you smoking when you came up with that one?" Why would they? In their minds every idea has merit, except the ones that are boring or involve eating a green leafy vegetable.

As we discussed at the outset, kids like to play and have fun; it helps free their minds to innovate. When we were young, we could create dozens of games to play with a ball, stick, or piece of rope. When we found a playground with a ball or any reasonable equipment, there was an unlimited set of options for having fun. As adults we tend to see each toy as having a particular purpose and a set way to be used. A ball can be thrown and caught, kicked, rolled, or struck with a bat, a tennis racket, or a golf club. But it is still a ball. Kids, on the other hand, create a million ways to play with a ball, including hiding it, spinning it, bouncing it off a wall or a car, painting it, dressing it up, putting

Figure 21. Some Kids' Innovations

Idea	Primary Benefit
The scissor comb	Enables you to trim your hair while you comb—to always keep it looking great.
Puddle shoes	Incorporate a magnifying glass into your shoes so you can see what you're stepping in in detail.
Food-resistant clothing	Reduces the amount of laundry to be done and eliminates the need to wear an unsightly bib.
Invisible training wheels	So no one will know you haven't learned to ride a bicycle without them yet.
Permanent chalk	Lets your perfect hopscotch course or other driveway drawings survive after a heavy rain.
Health club for toys	A place for your dolls and stuffed animals to exercise and keep their bodies in shape.
Instantly melting cheese	Allows you to make melted-cheese sandwiches right in the cafeteria at school.
Suntan lotion paints	Keeps great works of art from fading from too much exposure to the sun.
Coffee bird food	Keeps the birds awake and singing all the time.

it under their clothes to pretend that they are having a baby, and so on. We could say that adults don't do more on the playground because of the limits of our bodies, but it is more due to the limits of our imaginations and creativity (along with our energy).

The Challenge for Companies and Their Leaders

Practically every company today is talking about innovation and its role in business success. They mention it in press releases that hail their latest and greatest new products and services. They highlight it in annual reports to employees and shareholders. And they call for everyone in the organization to think "out of the box," in the hope that asking for new and better ideas will be enough to make a difference. If only it were that easy.

Unfortunately, most companies have great difficulty consistently innovating in those areas of their businesses that provide real competitive advantage. They fail because they neglect the two most important ingredients for corporate innovation (other than chocolate and cinnamon): the need to create the right environment to spur and nurture new ideas and the need to give their people the skills, time, and motivation to come up with the right ideas and turn them into new and improved products, services, and business practices. As with several other things we've discussed, it is a relatively straightforward equation to put down on paper:

$$\text{consistent and appropriate innovation } = \\ \text{a supportive environment}$$

(A place where people are encouraged and supported in their efforts to develop the right new ideas.)

+

the ability to think and act like a small child
(Rediscovering the thirteen childhood gifts.)

This equation is even simpler to grasp when we realize how interconnected the environment is to the way we are taught to think and act as adults in companies.

Ask a group of adults if they are creative and you will probably get a resounding "No!" from almost everyone. Most will tell you they have lost the knack for coming up with new ideas and doing experiments at the office or in the kitchen. By the time we enter the world of work, we have been trained to solve problems or create opportunities in a much more businesslike and analytical way. We use business plan and business case methodologies, SWOT analyses, best-case scenarios, and a host of other structured tools to figure out our options and how to proceed. We even have to police ourselves in brainstorming meetings so that we don't criticize or mock new ideas. And, as we noted in the last chapter, we rely on the principle of avoiding risk, by only trying things that we are comfortable with and that have little or no likelihood of failure. So when we are asked to come up with a new product or service, we quickly look to "create" something like what we have done before or just like what our competitors have already successfully done. While this is not exactly a starting point filled with great possibilities, it has been, up until now, a formula for getting by. We tell ourselves that it is as good as we can do in an environment filled with serious rules, constraints, quantified expectations, preconceived notions about good and bad ideas, inertia, limited resources, and somewhat severe penalties for screwing up.

If we want to change the way we behave and the results we get, we must first change the contexts we operate in. That means breaking a lot of the rules, eliminating many of the constraints, changing how we set expectations, being open to new and very different ideas, freeing up the right resources, and even rewarding people for making big and important mistakes. We also have to start at the top of the organization where leaders establish the environment for what is valued based on their words, actions, and what they reward. While innovation can occur at all levels of a company, senior management is responsible for focusing attention on its importance and the need to create a "culture" and "mindset" that encourages finding and developing the best ideas (see Figure 22). This sets the stage for motivating people and getting them to believe that the company is serious about their ideas.

We also need to think about the most appropriate opportunities for innovation in our businesses. These are likely to be tied directly to our vision and enhancing what already sets us apart. Too many companies think of innovation only in terms of creating new products and services. In fact, innovative thinking and action can help us add greater value and gain competitive advantage in practically all areas of business. Figure 23 presents the results of a recent survey in which we asked our customers to identify important opportunities for innovation.

To appreciate this more clearly, imagine the world of a small shoemaker in Maine in 1905 who needed to figure out a way to compete with the retail giants of his time. He began to think about what mattered most to consumers and knew in his gut that

---

Figure 22. Creating the Right Mind-Set

No rules
No boundaries
No preconceived notions
No rigid frameworks
No bad ideas
No fear
No endless meetings

---

they were really looking for products that offered high quality and value for their money. His creative response was to offer (i.e., invent) an unconditional guarantee of satisfaction as the best way to assure quality. The result of this innovative pledge is now a $5 billion-a-year business named after its founder, L.L. Bean.

But what is the first step in getting all of our people to think like L.L. Bean? One way is to ask all of our people to become the entrepreneurs of their own jobs and areas of responsibilities. To do this, we must give them the tools, guidance, resources, and freedom to look at the world very differently so they can come up with the big and small ideas that will dramatically improve their parts of the business. We also have to challenge and teach our people to rediscover their childhood gifts and how to think and act like small children—with enthusiastic desire for their best ideas to actually see the light of day. Then it becomes a matter of continuing to train the brain and senses to make new connections, change frames of references, delight in a dose of igno-

Figure 23. Opportunities for Innovation

Product and Service Innovation

developing better new products and services
enhancing existing products and services
reducing product/service development cost and time
reducing time to market

Business Process Innovation

improving product or service quality
reducing the cost of doing business and increasing
    profitability
reinventing customer service and satisfaction
strengthening employee recruitment and retention
making the most of investments in technology

Marketing Innovation

identifying and building new market opportunities
developing new ways to position and promote products
    and services
rethinking product and service pricing
redefining selling
reinventing distribution channels

Leadership and Management Innovation

developing and executing a winning vision and strategy
improving the way that the organization is structured and
    managed

(cont.)

Figure 23. Opportunities for Innovation (continued)

enhancing the organization's ability to innovate
    consistently
building effective teams and partnerships
strengthening communication inside and outside the
    organization
motivating people to leap tall buildings in a single bound
creating innovative incentive and reward systems
improving morale and having more fun

---

rance, open up to new things, and explore new worlds of possibilities. It's also a matter of making the time commitment to practice each day by encouraging brainstorming, exchanging ideas, and playing with secret ingredients.

Big Lesson #10

Creativity is the one key to making a real difference.

Summary

In a child's world, creativity is the natural order of things. As adults we must rediscover how to get out of the boxes we have built. Innovation is the name we give to a world of powerful possibilities. Given the right environment, skills, and motivation, we can all make some amazing salsa.

> *Children come into this world with a natural inclination to sing, to dance, to create.*
>
> SANDRA BROWN WILLIAMS

Lessons from the Sandbox

Creativity and Innovation

- Creativity is the one key to making a real difference.

- Be open to possibilities.

- A certain degree of ignorance is truly a virtue.

- Anything can go together with anything else if you have enough imagination and a bottle of Elmer's glue.

- Nothing is only as it seems.

- Everyone has enough creativity to help improve the company's performance and make a giant mess in the kitchen.

Just for Fun *and* Profit

Here are some things you can do today to rediscover the gift of creativity and innovation in order to improve your company's or business unit's bottom-line success.

Start by Unraveling a Slinky

When we were kids, we could come up with a million uses for almost anything we were given or found. As adults we have to work hard to stretch our minds. So a good place to start recapturing our childhood creativity is by taking an object like a Slinky (though you can use practically anything—e.g., an apple, a bedpan, etc.) and quickly make a list of all the things you could use it for. Try to come up with 20 or more unique ideas in less than five minutes.

Build a New Product

Ask everyone in your group to come up with an idea for a great new product. Then build working prototypes using odds and ends you find in your garages or workrooms at home. Try to use things that would not typically be used in making your type of product. Then have everyone bring their creations to the office and make a compelling case for the company's investment. Come up with creative "awards" for each idea and commit to keeping the best ones alive.

Proclaim a Salsa Day

Spend an entire day putting salsa on everything you eat. Then take notes and apply what you learn to growing your business. (You will be amazed at its great versatility.)

Part III

Belonging

Human beings are the only creatures that
allow their children to come home.

BILL COSBY

Now let's turn to the third part of our equation for growing—the way we fit in and found our place in the world around us.

As small children, our overriding life-goal was to belong. (Actually, the same thing applies to most adults, though they are not always as obvious in pursuing it.) As kids we were always looking for opportunities to play and interact with other people, participate in whatever they were doing, be accepted by them, and make valued contributions. We would try practically anything in order to get involved. When other people needed help with unpleasant chores, we were there with smiles. When older kids needed someone to sacrifice his or her body for an experiment, we were ready and willing. When a ball, pack of gum, or a small pet fell into a very small place, we were eager to crawl down to make the rescue. If these efforts didn't work, we would make so much noise and trouble that people would include us just to neutralize our behavior.

Belonging was more than just being involved. Once we won the right to participate, we quickly set our sights higher—looking for chances to involve others in what we wanted to do and promoting activities and causes we thought were important. We also focused on creating comfortable and secure places to anchor ourselves in a world filled with things we didn't understand, including an occasional monster, ghost, or mean person. These cozy places, filled with all of the right stuff, were safe harbors where we could be at our best. We also delighted in chances to accomplish things that were important to us and were quick to express our joy when our achievements were recognized and appreciated.

In the temporary and competitive world of business today, companies are trying to figure out how to find, keep, and motivate the best employees. They do this with an emphasis on money and rewards in the hope that people will do the jobs that need to get done. We often forget, however, that what most people want, more than anything else, is the chance to belong and make a lasting difference in something they value. Looking at how small children make themselves belong sheds a bright light on what we should do as companies to create the right environment for all of our employees and partners—an environment that rediscovers the basics of what it takes to contribute and be valued.

From Strange Noises to Complete Sentences

An important part of belonging is being able to communicate effectively. For most children, words become the best way to interact with others, let them know their needs, and expand their opportunities to participate in all of the exciting things going on around them. Between the ages of one and two, most small children make quantum leaps in their speaking skills. This new ability enables them to do a much better job of expressing themselves to a broader audience than just Mom, Dad, and the few other weirdos capable of decoding kids' initial seal-like sounds, gestures, and attention-getting actions. But it goes beyond simply communicating. Words, no matter how few, become the main currency for gaining a place at the table, in the tree house, or in the game.

When we were small children, language was clearly a work-in-progress. At first, we said only single words with priority given to those of one syllable. This was enough to get our basic needs met. When we said certain words like "food," "book," "head," "shoes," "mine," or "poop," most people around us knew exactly what was on our minds. "Food" meant we were hungry; "book" meant it would be great if someone would read to us; "head" meant we ran into something and could use an icepack; "shoe" meant we were eager to go outside to play; "mine" meant someone was messing with some of our favorite stuff (which was anything of ours). And "poop," . . . well, you get the picture. "Yes!" meant we liked whatever we were doing or were going to do, and "no" meant that we did not. An empathetic "No!" meant that if we didn't get our way, we would hold a sit-down (or lie-down) strike that could stop traffic at several of the world's busiest airports.

Other things were probably less obvious to the naked ear until we started to put our words together to form phrases and then sentences. This occurrence gave great cause for both celebration and concern. During the months leading up to this event, Mom and Dad had been busy planting the seeds of kind, considerate, and thoughtful conversation. To this end, they regularly repeated phrases like "I love you," "Thank you very much," "Can you please pass the vegetables?" "It is very nice of you to invite us," "It is a pleasure to be here," "You have a beautiful home," "I love your dinner plates and your choice of artwork," "Long live the free-enterprise system," and "I don't even notice your bald spot." This constant coaching was intended to transmit the most socially acceptable notions, prevent their public embarrassment, and enable us to win friends and influence potential enemies. But even with all of this prompting, we still managed to let out an occasional: "Stop it!" "You're bad!" "You're mean!" "I hate you!" "This is mine!" and

"That driver is a total idiot!" And each expression left our parents wondering aloud, "Who taught Junior how to say that?"

But we were only trying to fit in and figure out how to belong in a world that sent out so many conflicting signals. So we would eagerly copy the words, sentences, and even semi-disgusting bodily sounds of an older sibling if it put us in their good graces. After all, belonging—especially to our evolving peer group—was essential to our growth and development, and we were focused, enthusiastic, and urgent in our desire to succeed.

> *When I was born I was so surprised*
> *that I didn't talk for a year and a half.*
>
> GRACIE ALLEN

11

The Gift of Participation

To COMPETE SUCCESSFULLY in the future, companies will need to do a better job of getting all their people to participate in ways that make a difference.

Leading companies are learning new ways to get the most out of their people by sharing responsibility, authority, and information. Under the banners of empowerment, teamwork, and diversity they are acknowledging the important contributions that everyone has to make to ensure success.

Small children are veritable wizards when it comes to getting involved and making a real difference. Their lives provide a dynamic model for getting everyone to participate and share their special gifts in the name of top- and bottom-line performance.

Great discoveries and improvements invariably involve the cooperation of many minds.

ALEXANDER GRAHAM BELL

"What is REAL?" asked the Rabbit one day, when they were lying side by side near the nursery fender, before Nana came to tidy the room.

"Does it mean having things that buzz inside you and a stick-out handle?"

"Real isn't how you are made," said the Skin Horse.

"It's a thing that happens to you. When a child loves you for a long, long time, not just to play with, but REALLY loves you, then you become Real."

MARGERY WILLIAMS,
THE VELVETEEN RABBIT, 1922

If you grew up with brothers and sisters, you no doubt recall many remarkable moments you shared together. Whether they were pleasant or unpleasant at the time, most seem quite humorous in retrospect. At an early age, in particular, small kids eagerly try to participate in their older siblings' activities and do whatever it takes to be involved. Unfortunately, many big kids don't want to be bothered by a small child who might play with their things, cramp their style, annoy their friends, mess up their rooms even more, or report their activities back to the authorities (i.e., Mom or Dad). But the younger child is usually quite persistent, and often is willing to do just about anything to get in the good graces of his or her brother or sister. This includes being subjected to a range of tests and experiments.

"But She Asked Me to Cut!"

It should have been clear to everyone involved that something mischievous was taking place. After all, it is impossible for two sisters to be quiet for that long, unless secret and clandestine activities were part of the agenda. But as far as their unsuspecting parents knew, the girls were reading books and playing with the dollhouse—big sister's door was shut just to give them a bit of privacy. One might have assumed, in a rare moment of parental bliss, that the total silence equated to a magical bonding that should not be interrupted.

In the privacy of big sister's room, however, some very exciting work was going on, involving a willing subject, a good deal of concentration, a pair of scissors, and the need for a good explanation.

Someone older had decided to give someone younger a special haircut, and after twenty minutes of enthusiastic though untrained snipping, it was time to face an adoring public. Big sister was not particularly eager to come out. But there was very little hair left to cut, and little sister was a bit anxious to move on to the next unplanned act of involvement in her day. Needless to say, when she emerged from the room and walked downstairs looking like a reject from heavy metal night on MTV, Mom and Dad instantly went into shock and quickly tried to find out what had happened.

All parties came front and center to discuss the important topics of appearance, career planning, and growing up in harmony. "Does anyone have any idea what happened to your sister?" seemed like a good starting point. "What do you mean?" was the logical first response. Then a long "Ummm . . ." on both sides, followed by, "Does she look a bit different to you now than when she first arrived in your room to read a book twenty minutes ago?" "Oh, you mean that?" big sister asked. "Yes, that's precisely what we mean!" "Well, she brought me the scissors and said 'Cut,' which I assumed meant she wanted a haircut." "Uh-huh . . ." "And," big sister continued, "she didn't complain while I was doing it *and* she looked at herself in the mirror *and* she didn't say that she didn't like it. And . . ." then a long pause, "It's not the best haircut I've ever seen." Finally something they could all agree on. Dad continued, "She looks like she just arrived from a planet where personal appearance is not a major concern." "I think she's kind of cute like this," big sister added, hoping to diffuse things. "Without hair on her head?" Mom inquired, not knowing whether to laugh or cry. "Well it *is* summer," big sister noted, "so it is is better to have short hair, isn't it?"

So much for trying to reason with a six-year-old. Interestingly, the younger sister was as happy as can be. Not that she thought it was a great haircut. But she had achieved her overriding objective of bonding with her big sister and participating in a meaningful way. She didn't really comprehend how silly she looked. Even a look in the mirror did nothing to sidetrack her successful partnering. After all, don't you ever wonder what small kids think when they look at themselves in the mirror?

Anyway, the minor catastrophe was resolved by a quick trip to the beauty salon where little sister got a crew cut to even out the damage. Mom and Dad partnered to come up with an explanation that could be told to the world at large. And big sister realized that little kids are all right and cutting hair requires some actual training.

A Small Child's Guide to Participating

When we were kids, we wanted to be involved in almost everything going on around us. The thought that other people might be doing interesting stuff and having fun without us was more than we could bear. Because we didn't want to miss anything worth doing, we quickly developed our skills of scanning the universe for activity, hovering, listening to (and possibly interrupting) other people's conversations, and injecting ourselves into those activities we wanted to be part of. We were eager and willing to pay the price for participation.

It's not as if other people didn't ever want us to participate in their activities or we didn't have anything valuable to contribute. In fact, sometimes we were actually sought out by others who recognized our unique abilities or willingness to try almost anything. We shouldn't forget that no family event could have proceeded without us. We, however, were most interested in participating in those activities that required our own initiatives to get involved.

Our first line of offense in gaining participation was simply to appear and hope that our cuteness would carry the day. This was not a bad tactic for a lot of things in which an extra body couldn't hurt and secrecy was not an issue. "I promise not to bother you," was our likely comment in some intelligible form, followed by, "I will just sit here quietly and not make a sound. You won't even notice that I'm here." Of course, this was a total impossibility for a small child, but certainly worth a try. If we were not rebuffed, we would usually find a comfortable way to fit in or find a spot where we could be part of things without making waves.

Once we felt accepted, we might have tried to stretch the bounds of our participation by asking, "Can I try?" Many times others were willing to let us. We also offered to help in order to participate and get attention. "I'll carry your ball" or "I'll clean up your mess" were the types of things that usually got a favorable response. If help was not needed at that exact moment, we made it clear we would be available to help when the need did arise.

When a simple straightforward offer to help didn't carry the day, we volunteered to do the dirty work no one else wanted to do. We must have felt that doing the impossible would win over the hearts and minds of others and earn us the right to do the good stuff. From our perspective, doing the undesirable jobs was still participating and that was OK with us. "I can climb through that small opening in the fence to get your Frisbee!" "I can sneak into the house past Mom and Dad and get the money on the table that you want to use to buy an ice cream!" "I can sit still and not make a sound while you cut my hair!" And so on.

When all else failed, we had the uncanny ability to become big pests and wear down other people until they let us participate. We quickly learned, however, that this tactic rarely put us in anyone's good graces.

Par-tic-i-pat-ing, v. *the act of joining or sharing with others in order to do something special*

We were also skillful at initiating things and involving other people in what we wanted to do. "Want to draw a picture with me?" or "kick a ball?" or "play in a puddle?" or "listen to music?" or "read a book?" We knew if we could figure out something worth doing, others might be willing to join in.

Our desire to involve other people was based on our recognition at an early age that different people brought different skills, ideas, games, and stuff (books, toys, dogs, etc.) to the table or sandbox. Other people meant more choices and opportunities to get involved in something fun. Diversity, a very hot topic in business today, was never an issue for us as kids. We judged people based on whether they were nice or mean, which was largely based on their willingness to include us or their desire to positively participate in what we were doing.

As kids we also wanted to participate in a special way—one-on-one—with people whom we cared about. The chance to have someone special all to yourself was awesome and provided a way to be in a quiet spotlight of participation and undivided attention.

Kids want to participate because they have the burning desire to belong, get attention, be accepted, and be viewed as having valuable contributions to make. Participation also gives kids the chance to learn new skills and make new friends. Participation provides a perfect forum for learning and growing.

The Challenge for Companies and Their Leaders

As adults we are also driven to belong, participate, and make a difference, even though we aren't always as clever (or as cute) as a small child in trying to make it happen. We arrive on the scene with a lot of enthusiasm, energy, and hope, eager to put our skills to good use. We arrive with also a bit of apprehension as to whether or not we will fit in. But we are often willing to take on the dirty jobs in order to be part of the team and gain a better seat and a bigger voice at the table.

In some respects we are most valuable to our companies or organizations when we first arrive on the scene. As the new kids in town, we bring our own fresh eyes, experiences, ideas, and perspectives. If we are encouraged to share them early on and question things we don't understand, we can be an important check for the organization as it seeks to be its best. Unfortunately, most companies don't see the benefits or take the time to capture this good stuff.

In other respects we are most valuable once we have gotten up to speed and can apply what we know to what needs to be done. As we get to know the organization better, we can find the right opportunities to really add value. In either case, we must step forward to offer our best as the organization steps forward to encourage it. That is where too many companies fail to understand and capitalize on the gift of participation and what it means to get the most out of everyone.

For example, assume that everyone in your organization has a valuable contribution to make from the moment they arrive until their last day with you. Now, how do you tap it? How do you inspire everyone to do their best and be willing to help? You know people will sign up to participate and help if something is worth doing. So you need to make sure, as was discussed earlier, that you are focused on doing something special and giving everyone a clear understanding of his or her role in making things happen and doing the best job possible.

Participation comes with requirements and responsibilities on the part of individuals and companies. As individuals we need to be willing to step up and get involved, learn new skills, and offer something of value, beginning with simply being willing to help. As companies we should see to it that everyone has something valuable to contribute. We need to create a place in which everyone has the chance to be accepted, be valued, and belong. We should also see that the variety of contributions is powerful. To compete successfully, we need all of our people with all of their perspectives to stir the pot—especially the ones who think like small kids. Like small kids, we should only be concerned with whether people are nice or mean and whether they can make us better as companies.

We also have to do a better job of engaging people and getting them to participate quickly in something important that they can put their talents and passion into. A good starting point is to ask *them* what they can contribute and what excites them, rather than go with what we think we need them to do right now. Getting them to step forward also means giving them clear guidance on our objectives as an organization, then providing the opening, encouragement, and support for them to succeed. We also should find out how they want to belong and participate, so we can make sure they can mesh with the way we operate.

A part of engaging people is giving them special time with mentors who can teach, coach, and inspire them. The ability to bond with someone whom we respect and who can teach us things we want and need to know is critical to belonging and participating in a meaningful way. It is also an asset to our organization because it strengthens our talent and leadership base and forges the basis for longer-term commitment.

Big Lesson #11

When we have a chance to participate and use our special gifts, we can do amazing things.

What is a home without children?
Quiet.

HENNY YOUNGMAN

Summary

When we were small kids we did whatever we could to get involved, belong, and make a difference. As adults in companies we need to do a better job of encouraging everyone to participate and contribute. Participation is the name we give to being a valued part of something worth doing. We can get a real haircut when the other important stuff is done.

Lessons from the Sandbox

Participation

- When we have a chance to participate and use our special gifts, we can do amazing things.

- It's never a bad idea to ask if you can help.

- Be willing to do almost anything for a chance to participate.

- There is power in a diversity of people and ideas.

- Having a mentor can improve our learning and the value of our participation.

- Never assume that an older sister or a coworker is an expert with a scissors.

Just for Fun *and* Profit

Here are some things you can do today to rediscover the gift of participation in order to improve your company's or business unit's bottom-line success.

Get Involved in Something New

Commit to getting involved in a new activity, either at work or in your social or civic life. Pick something important to you and develop a game plan for participating and making a real contribution. You might start by offering to help in a way that is needed. Then look for the chance to bring your special skills to bear.

Compose a Song

Get your team together to write a song about what it takes to involve everyone and tap their special gifts. To make your job easier, you can tie your lyrics to the music of a popular song or TV-show theme. Then create an opportunity to sing it and make sure everyone has a valued role to play. This is a simple way to focus on an important issue, have fun, and build an even greater sense of teamwork and camaraderie.

Become a Mentor

Look for the opportunity to become a mentor to someone in your company or a student at a local high school or college. But make sure to check your ego at the door so you can really make a difference. You will be surprised at how much you learn from sharing your knowledge and experience and helping to develop the best in others.

12

The Gift of
Cozy Places

To compete successfully in the future, companies will
need to create and nurture safe places for people and
their ideas.

The workplace is undergoing dramatic changes as companies try to build environments that nurture productivity
and creativity while reducing the cost of doing business.
But how do we create settings where people can really be at their
best, even if they won't be with us forever?

Small children have an uncanny ability to turn any place into
a setting for learning and growth. They can teach us a lot about
what it takes to make workplaces more enjoyable, stimulating,
comfortable, safe, and profitable.

We will try to create conditions where persons could come together in a spirit of teamwork, and exercise to their heart's desire their technological capacity.

AKIO MORITA, FOUNDER,
SONY CORPORATION

They flew over the Charles River.

"This is better," quacked Mr. Mallard. "That island looks like a nice quiet place, and it's only a little way from the Public Garden."

"Yes," said Mrs. Mallard, remembering the peanuts. "That looks like just the right place to hatch ducklings."

So they chose a cozy spot among the bushes near the water and settled down to build their nest. And only just in time, for now they were beginning to molt. All their old wing feathers started to drop out, and they would not be able to fly again until the new ones grew in.

ROBERT MCCLOSKEY, *MAKE WAY
FOR DUCKLINGS*, 1941

When we were kids, we created a lot of very special places to hide in, hang out in, or just get comfortable in. These were our own corners of the world where we could accomplish small and great tasks or simply get ready for whatever came next. In our bedrooms we fashioned a bunch of special "work" areas—in bed, under the bed, in the closet, in a corner, or at a desk if we had one. We also had a corner of almost every other room in the house. We even had the area under the dining room table where we could retreat to when we got tired of the meal or conversation. The backyard, if we had one, offered many prime spots to work out of, which might have included a sandbox, a play set, or even a treehouse. We had the car, especially the back of the station wagon where we could camp out or hold court. We also had a place behind the garage or under a tree, a tent we could put up, or an inflatable swimming pool. All could be made perfect with a bit of interior or exterior decorating.

The Tooth Fairy!

"What are you up to?" I asked our five-year-old daughter, amazed and curious about the major public works project underway on her bed. "I'm making a perfect cozy place," she replied, "just in case my special visitor comes tonight." "Special visitor?" I wondered aloud. Was there a special visitor stopping by whom I had not marked on my calendar? "You know, Papa, the tooth fairy. I'm losing this tooth any minute now and I have to be ready." "But she'll come in the middle of the night when you're asleep." "I know. But I have to be comfortable to lose a tooth."

By now the tooth was hanging by a proverbial string, and as she worked to create a great cozy place, she was also working very diligently to get it out. But the evening was mostly spent making sure everything was in perfect condition. Pillows just so, special blankets arranged to provide a tentlike space, all of her favorite dolls and stuffed animals in their places, favorite books neatly arranged at the end of the bed, a water bottle close at hand, just the right amount of light, and so on—all to set the mood for one very special tooth to come out and one very special visitor to make her appearance.

"Is there really a tooth fairy?" Sara asked, hoping to get clear confirmation that this was not another adult hoax.

"Definitely," I replied. "And she is a very busy person who rarely gets an evening off."

"But how does she know I'm losing a tooth tonight?"

"That's a perfectly good question. You see, she looks out over the world with special eyes and special radar that zoom in on teeth."

"And where does she live that she can see all the boys and girls with loose teeth?"

"I think that she lives outside of Cleveland," I answered. (Remember, I am a trained geographer.)

"Where's that?"

"It's close enough to get here as soon as your tooth comes out."

"But what if she forgets?"

> *"Don't worry, sweetheart, I have taken precautions and sent
> her an E-mail early this morning with a map of our
> neighborhood."*
> "Are you sure, Papa?"
> *"Yup, I'm sure!"*

At 8:32 P.M. eastern standard time, halfway through Chapter
6 of *Stuart Little* by E. B. White, and under intense pressure
applied by a small girl, an extremely small tooth decided to call it
quits and tumbled down onto one of the twenty pillows arranged
carefully in the girl's bed. Our daughter then made a rare request
for the story to end and the lights to go out, so she could fall asleep
and the magic could happen in her perfect cozy place.

A Small Child's Guide to Cozy Places

When we were small children, we created cozy places to help us
belong and perform at our best. We also created them to help us
cope with a set of fears we began to experience at a relatively early
age, including fear of the dark, fear of being away from Mom and
Dad, and fear of monsters or other scary things underneath the
bed or in the closet. Fortunately, the tooth fairy opened up the
possibility that wonderful creatures, as opposed to scary ones,
might come into our room in the middle of the night while we
were sleeping.

The ability to create cozy places anywhere and at any time
gave us a measure of control over the world around us. Even when
we left the secure confines of our own homes we would, with
slightly more effort, create the perfect spot for getting things

done. We would find the best corner of a friend's or relative's house, most likely behind the sofa, in an alcove, or in the dog's bed. If we were boys (and had the transportation gene) we would bring our bags of trucks, cars, and other vehicles into the middle of a room or under the table at a restaurant and sit contentedly until dessert was served, as we solved the world's growing traffic congestion problem. On an airplane we would sit down on the floor nestled amid the carry-on luggage, drawing pictures, playing fifty-two-card pickup, spilling our drinks, or turning our little bag of pretzels into bread crumbs. When we got really cozy, we would untie everyone else's shoelaces.

Behind all of this effort was an honest desire to get comfortable, since we knew from the earliest age this was essential to getting things done. Creating a cozy place is one of the signature events that mark the magical world of toddlers. As small kids we instinctively knew how to do it—anywhere.

Co-zy Places, n. *safe and comfortable places in which to rest, think, and make great things happen*

I remember recently watching a small two-year-old girl as she walked into the gift shop at a local hospital. Upon seeing a wall filled with stuffed animals, she walked over, carrying her own special blanket, and started talking to them. She then touched them; she moved just enough of them over so she could sit on the shelf next to them; then she took a couple of the animals she had just removed and put them on her lap and in her arms. Finally, she looked up and smiled, knowing she had quickly made a perfect cozy place. Small kids can even create an instant cozy place by squatting, a posture they can hold for several days at a time, which is impossible for an adult (other than a baseball catcher) to do for more than a few seconds without requiring the assistance of a physical therapist.

The place, however, was just part of the equation. As kids we also needed to have the right stuff. While there was some difference in what we might take depending on if we were boys or girls, there were some key ingredients that no cozy place would be without. To a small child, a perfect cozy place was a spot that was not too big and that had the special blanket (the real-life security blanket), some special friends (i.e., stuffed animals or even a real animal, dolls, toys, etc.), a pillow or two or even twenty, some books, a snack, and a beverage. Some kids would add a tent or a canopy to cover them and make things even more cozy.

When we were small kids, we were also keenly aware of the need to make other people comfortable and would graciously invite them into our special places and surround them with the appropriate accoutrements. At certain times, the presence of other people made our cozy places seem even more secure and safe.

Cozy places were an important part of our routine and the perfect spot to take a nap or at least unwind. Left to our own devices there we could recharge our batteries and shake off any less-than-pleasant tendencies that might be stirring. When we sensed the impending arrival of our "evil twin," we often sought out or created new cozy places to cushion us and prevent us from going over the edge of social impropriety.

The Challenge for Companies and Their Leaders

During the past three years our company asked more than 10,000 businesspeople where and when they are most creative. The results, while not particularly scientific, are very enlightening. It turns out, people in companies of all sizes rarely have their most brilliant ideas at the office. In fact, when asked *where* they were most creative, less than 3 percent of respondents answered, "At work." The most common responses were

1. on vacation   18%

2. while driving a car   14%

3. taking a walk in the woods 12%

4. in the shower   11%

5. working in the yard   9%

6. with friends   8%

With "work" coming in a distant ninth, just behind sitting someplace quiet (with or without a favorite beverage).

Asked *when* they were most creative, over 70 percent of people said either early in the morning or sometime in the evening. Again, these are not the prime times when most of us are in the office.

These findings have important implications for companies, because they indicate that the one place where we are being paid to get comfortable and use the gray matter between our ears is one place where few of us actually do so. In fact, while many corporations talk about creating great work environments that nurture their people, it does not seem to be happening for most folks at most businesses. The bottom-line cost of this is probably staggering.

As we discussed in Chapter 10, companies need to do a better job of creating places in which all of their people are challenged and inspired to innovate. But there is much more to it. As adults in companies, we need cozy places now just as much as we did when we were small kids—but for slightly different reasons. We need them, first and foremost, as refuges from the craziness of each day, places to hide and unwind, to regroup, and to get our acts together. We also need them as places to do our best thinking, where we can be as creative as possible. This suggests filling them with some of the important trappings of those special places in which we really are at our best, and being surrounded by people who bring out the very best in us. It also suggests making the broader workplace more comfortable for thinking, wondering, testing, playing, and trying new things.

The importance of comfort and safety cannot be overlooked if we want people to do their best work for us. Not unlike kids, adults in companies have legitimate fears. Not fears of the dark, but of being left in the dark. Not fears of Mom and Dad going away, but of leaders who won't communicate effectively with us. Not fears of monsters under the bed, but of unknown competitors who could sneak in and take over our customers and markets, and of unexpected takeovers that could jeopardize what we have worked so hard to build up. We need to work together to address these fears, and creating a cozy place for mind and body is an important part of how we can cope and prosper.

How do we make this happen as quickly as possible, when today's business world won't give us much time to make everyone feel comfortable? We can start by asking people what they would like to do to adapt their environments in order to create their own cozy place (or places) given the constraints of our places of business. We can also ask them what resources and support they will need. Then we should make special time for them to recharge their batteries, focus their creative energies, take walks in the woods if necessary, and even take naps or have milk and cookies, all in support of getting great work done.

The precedent for this type of thinking is already being set by many leading companies like GTE, Chase Manhattan Bank, Discovery Communications, IBM, Life Technologies, and Eli Lilly (to mention just a few) that have begun to focus attention on the importance of helping employees to balance their work and personal lives. The growing "worklife" movement is redefining the way we work and the nature of the workday in significant ways. We now have flex-time, job sharing, cross-training, telecommuting, casual dress, on-site childcare, parental leave, and a host of other programs that are designed to show respect for employees as complete people and not just workers. We also have special events that are designed to show appreciation and build a sense of spirit and commitment. We even have a growing number of innovative training programs that help employees to develop not only their work skills but their skills in balancing their lives. So the idea of emphasizing the importance of comfort in the workplace should make perfect sense.

But we don't spend enough time thinking about the concept of cozy places in the success of companies. We have all but admitted that we live in a temporary world in which jobs and loyalty are relatively short-term things (unless we can tie someone up with stock options). So we really need the ability to quickly make people feel comfortable, involved, eager, and willing to give us their best brainpower. And not just four walls and an in-box. If that means a blanket, some pillows, some toys, a few stuffed animals, and a chance to listen to classical music with a beverage of your choosing, it is a pretty good price to pay.

Big Lesson #12

Cozy and comfortable places are the best spots for creating magic.

Summary

When we were young, we knew that being comfortable was essential to doing our very best work. As adults we need to rediscover that importance again. Cozy places are the name we give to the old and inviting chair where our best ideas can flourish—a place to welcome customers, colleagues, shareholders, and any other special visitors from Cleveland.

> *The quickest way for a parent to get a child's attention is to sit down and look comfortable.*
>
> LANE OLINGHOUSE

Lessons from the Sandbox

Cozy Places

- Cozy and comfortable places are the best spots for creating magic.

- It is good to know where and when you are at your best, and to spend as much time there as possible.

- It's much easier to be productive when there aren't any monsters under your desk.

- When all else fails, a familiar blanket is a good friend to have.

- Never underestimate the value of a well-timed nap.

Just for Fun *and* Profit

Here are some things you can do today to rediscover the gift of cozy places in order to improve your company's or business unit's bottom-line success.

Figure Out Where You Are at Your Best

Think about where and when you are at your best and the key characteristics of those times and places. You might even want to take some pictures or make a sketch to keep it fresh in your mind. Then try to figure out how to incorporate those "trappings" into your work space to support the critical things that you are responsible for doing. You can compare notes with your colleagues and then develop a plan of action.

Create Your Own Cozy Space

Now take your best ideas and create the perfect cozy place where you can be at your best. Do it at work, if possible, or at home if that's the only option. Or find a place outside to use as a good retreat. Then create a regular routine for using this place to anchor yourself and energize your thinking.

Give Your People a Greater Sense of Comfort

Give all of your team members something that demonstrates your commitment to creating the best work environment for them. It can be a special pillow for their offices and meetings, a stuffed animal, a stress ball, a Slinky, or a bench outside under a tree.

13

The Gift of
Accomplishment

To compete successfully in the future, companies will
need to inspire all of their employees to accomplish
great and small things.

Companies today are asking more and more from their people as they raise the bar on the results required to succeed.
A big part of the equation, however, is providing a wider
range of new and innovative incentives and rewards in order to
increase initiative, commitment, and bottom-line results.

Small children focus on accomplishing new things and being
recognized and applauded for jobs well done. Watching them in
action provides valuable insight into how to encourage and reward
people in order to get the best out of them.

*Outstanding leaders go out of the way
to boost the self-esteem of their person-
nel. If people believe in themselves, it's
amazing what they can accomplish.*

SAM WALTON, FOUNDER, WAL-MART

I can tie my shoelace

I can comb my hair

I can wash my hands and face

And dry myself with care.

I can brush my teeth, too

And button up my frocks;

I can say, How do you do?

And put on both my socks.

FROM *MOTHER GOOSE*

Few, if any, events in our lives as small children were surrounded by as much attention, interest, coaching, and encouragement as learning to go to the bathroom. Between the ages of two and three, most of us begin to realize there is a much better way to do our "business"—i.e., a way that affords far greater independence, fewer rashes, and an awful lot of praise. At about the same time, our coaches, typically Mom and Dad, begin to do lots of homework to pave the way for the big event. They ask their elders, network with peers, read all the leading books and periodicals, and even take courses on parenting and the power of positive discipline. Their objective is to free themselves from the burdens of having to clean up dirty diapers and carry around a diaper bag (which over time comes to hold enough stuff to cover a month-long vacation in Tahiti).

"I Did It!"

During our thirty-month checkup with the pediatrician, he asked if our daughter was potty trained. We responded that she had shown some interest a few months earlier but had regressed to the security of her diaper. As we left the office, we looked at each other and began to wonder if we were failing as parents and somehow slowing down her long-term growth and development.

As her third birthday approached along with her three-year checkup, my wife and I began to feel even more unskilled as parents. A quick survey of other parents at preschool confirmed that our team was falling a bit behind in the race to do bodily functions like a big kid. All our encouragement, reading potty-time books, and explaining the finer points of doing a "Number 2" (as my parents call it to this day) were not producing results.

It was time to take more drastic action. So without any further ado, we hooked up our home computer to the Internet and began to surf day and night for the answer. As you might recall, the early days of public access to the Web were a hit-or-miss affair of imperfect search engines leading to uneven information. We did, however, find a site from one of the most popular parenting magazines, and quickly made our way to the toilet-training chat room to see how others in our predicament were handling the stress.

I recall one evening when my wife sat down at the computer and began to read the advice of other parents. I also recall being amazed at how many people actually wanted to share their issues and ideas with total strangers whose only common bond was poop. There she sat, scrolling through each message and giving me feedback with each new solution.

> "I can't believe they would do that."
> "That's the dumbest idea I have ever heard."
> "That's what some of the books say."
> "That's OK, but it wouldn't work for us."
> "They can't be serious."
> "They shouldn't do that."
> "They call themselves parents?"
> "Clever but impractical."
> "It's got to be illegal."
> Then finally:
> "Perfect! This one will work!"

The method in question was so simple that Pavlov himself would have been amazed. It involved promising a piece of candy for every successful poop on the potty. Given that our daughter loved candy and at least seemed curious about the potty, it couldn't help but work. This was a brilliant idea, we said to ourselves. Even if it was suggested by a total stranger from Teaneck, New Jersey, it was elegant, simple, and only slightly habit-forming. So, armed with a small basket of chocolate, we sat down next to our daughter one evening and proposed the game (i.e., the bribe). I preferred to think of it as a business arrangement; compensation in exchange for specified services, i.e., a poop in the potty. After all, while we didn't mean to rush her, we were eager to move on to the next phase of parenting.

It worked like a charm. Upon the first success, our daughter smiled a giant smile and said simply, "I did it!" We responded that we were very proud of her and asked her if she was proud of herself. It worked so well that our daughter began to go potty all the time. With each subsequent success, she smiled a bigger smile and said, "I did it again!" We always responded with more pride and asked her what it was like to work hard to accomplish something important (without having her go into all of the details). For a short period of time, she was probably doing more Number 2s on the potty, or anywhere for that matter, than any other creature on the planet. With each effort, she got plenty of encouragement.

Within a few weeks, pooping became old news except for a modest amount of ongoing encouragement and praise, and the occasional "Uh-ohs" when we missed the target. The latter are, of course, to be expected when learning any new, complex, and important skill.

A Small Child's Guide to Accomplishment

When we were young, we had so much to learn and so much to accomplish. Each day brought a set of new challenges that we took on with great enthusiasm and energy. Some of these challenges involved learning very practical skills that enabled us to navigate our environment with greater ease. Other challenges involved learning social skills that made it easier for us to participate, fit in, make friends, and belong. Whatever the case, learning any new skill brought with it a great sense of accomplishment.

When we were small children, we delighted in accomplishing new things and would show our joy with huge smiles and the simple words "I did it!" spoken with pride and amazement. Whether it was figuring out how to clap our hands, standing up for the first time, putting a basketball in a two-foot-tall basket, learning to count to ten and then twenty, figuring out how to eat with a fork and spoon, memorizing the alphabet and then singing a song from *The Sound of Music*, climbing up an entire flight of stairs without help, or, later on, learning to read a book, the personal satisfaction of accomplishing something of value was simply beyond comparison.

Before the age of one, most of us could clap our hands, and we took great pleasure in using this particular skill. We clapped whenever other people did, when we heard music playing, when someone said "Yea!" "Bravo!" or "Good job!", and we clapped whenever the spirit moved us. This simple skill could always get a quick and encouraging response from our adoring public. It was also one of the first things we learned to do that we consciously were very proud of. And, in short order we would learn to clap to show our appreciation and to participate in lots of funny nursery rhymes, including "patty-cake." Once this sense of accomplishment came, there was no turning back.

Continuing to accomplish things worth doing was tied in large part to the encouragement we received. While we loved to do new things, we also loved to be spurred on by others whose opinions and support we valued, and to have them recognize and acknowledge the new leaps and bounds our minds and bodies were making. This support helped build our self-esteem and inspired us to take on new challenges with confidence that we would succeed. Can you remember the first time you received a standing ovation? It probably wasn't after your first piano recital, nor after your first goal in a soccer game, nor the time you spelled *ubiquitous* in a spelling bee, nor after your acceptance for the "Citizen of the Year" award from the local chamber of commerce. No, it was probably the first time that you clapped, stood up, or pooped on the potty. You can bet that Mom, Dad, Grandma, Grandpa, and the assembled siblings were on their feet screaming for an encore. You can also bet it left a wonderfully indelible mark on your ability to grow, develop, and try other new things.

Achiev-ing, v.   *the act of accomplishing something worth doing*

Accomplishment often required the appropriate use of incentives. This was particularly true when something was hard to do, took a long time to master, or wasn't exactly what we wanted to get done. Someone with influence had to figure out how to entice our interest and elicit our support. This involved understanding what would motivate us to do certain types of things, creating the right set of incentives to spur the desired actions, and tying the incentives to our performance (or at least to our effort toward the goal). Sound familiar? You have probably dealt with the same situation at work at least ten times in the past month. But it is safe to say that there is nothing like negotiating with a small child. The big battle for parents is to make sure the incentives are also tied to the big hairy goal of growth rather than the promotion of tooth decay. Candy and ice cream would, in the best of circumstances, give way to reading books, going to the library, visiting a museum, walking the dog, or getting some exercise in the park.

The Challenge for Companies and Their Leaders

As adults we too are driven to learn new skills and accomplish things worth doing. We hope our companies will value our contributions. We even hope, though we don't use those words exactly, that they will seek to build our self-esteem and confidence so we will commit to achieving even more and making more of a difference. As humans of any age, our overriding desire is to be able to smile and say "I did it!" with pride, joy, and even a little bit of amazement. Fortunately, that's what most companies need us to do.

But somewhere along the way to that straightforward objective, most companies get lost. They also quickly equate the wrong things with getting the right results. So consider for a second what it would take to get everyone in your company to leap tall buildings in single bounds, to come up with great new ideas that dramatically improve your performance, or to treat the customers so well that they would pay practically anything for your products and services. It would probably take many of the things brought up throughout this book. But at a gut level, much of the answer revolves around giving people the support, encouragement, and sense of belonging they need to accomplish new and important things. Recognizing people as unique individuals with special gifts to share is also essential.

We often make the mistake in business of thinking that everyone is motivated by the same things and that those things revolve primarily around money. Raise the level of the financial reward and we can raise the level of our employees' performance. Hold out a bigger carrot and someone will work around the clock to get the job done. Beat the competitor's best offer and we can keep our best people for a while longer. Money talks or employees walk. It's a sad statement and not a particularly good formula for growing a company over the long haul.

What if we changed the equation to one in which the core principle was giving people as many opportunities as possible to say "I did it!" for accomplishments great and small? What if we supported them by encouraging their efforts, acknowledging their achievements, and praising their commitments to doing great work? This really is what it means to belong and to achieve something of value. We have the ability to make this happen regularly for everyone in our organizations.

We begin by making clear our expectations, and working together to set the right metrics for achieving them. Then we define our role in helping our people to succeed. In other words, we let people know what is important, give them the tools to get it done, and show our willingness to have them put their own added value (style, energy) into the equation. Then we tailor our incentives to meet the specific needs and interests of every individual. Just as we wouldn't take twenty-five children into a shoe store and buy them all the same pair of shoes—in the same style, color, and size—we shouldn't offer all our employees the same incentives and assume that they fit everyone. The smarter thing would be to ask each person what it would take to get them to do great things. Then, within the constraints of our resources, we can tailor packages that meet their bottom lines. We should think more broadly about a range of incentives including chances to work on important things; greater visibility; support from mentors; access to training, resources, expertise, and facilities; chances to explore the world in search of answers, and chances to achieve greater balance in their lives, as well as reasonable financial rewards. We should also focus on our company as a place to accomplish great things, learn, and grow—a place to make a real difference and be appreciated, applauded, and occasionally given candy for an effort made or a job well done.

Big Lesson #13

Nothing is more powerful than the gift of accomplishment.

Summary

When we were young, we delighted in accomplishing something worth doing. As adults we need to rediscover the joy of doing new and important things. Accomplishment is the name we give to what matters most on the road to personal and business success.

Success comes in a can . . . "I can!"

WALLY "FAMOUS" AMOS

Lessons from the Sandbox

Accomplishment

- Nothing is more powerful than the gift of accomplishment.

- The goal of every person is to belong and to make a real difference.

- Everyone is different and incentives should reflect what makes them tick and excel.

- The most important words are "I did it!"

- The second most important words are "Great job!"

- Never underestimate the power of chocolate.

Just for Fun *and* Profit

Here are some things you can do today to rediscover the gift of accomplishment in order to improve your company's or business unit's bottom-line success.

Take Stock of Your Accomplishments

Take the time to think about what you have already accomplished and what you hope to accomplish in the months and years ahead. Then think about what will motivate you to succeed and what support, encouragement, and resources will help you to get it done.

Create a Pool of Special Incentives

Sit down with your team members and think creatively about incentives that would spur them to make great things happen. Cast a wide net, but focus squarely on linking the incentives to your critical business objectives. Then try them out to see how they work. If you are like most people, you will be pleasantly surprised and excited about the ideas your people come up with.

Give Everyone a Standing Ovation

Commit to giving each person in your organization a standing ovation during the next month for something they did to improve your bottom-line performance.

Conclusion

To COMPETE SUCCESSFULLY in the future, companies will need to innovate, learn, and grow at the speed of life in a world that is changing faster than we ever imagined possible.

> *We didn't lose the game; we just ran out of time.*
>
> VINCE LOMBARDI

Rediscovering the Keys to Business Success

Time flies. Technologies converge. Paradigms shift. New markets open at the drop of a hat. New competitors appear at the blink of an eye. New ideas and new business models are everywhere. Simply running fast means falling farther behind. We are told we need to innovate and grow or our companies will perish. We are also told we need to lead change, manage knowledge, and break free of the old ways of doing things. But how do we jump on a train that is moving too fast for most of us to see?

When we were kids, it was a lot easier to deal with such monumental changes. After all, we came into the world knowing practically nothing about it, except for the sound of our family's voices and possibly the bark of a dog or the shriek of a siren off in the distance. We could have folded our tents right then and there. We didn't, because we must have known we would figure things out by sticking to our own innate formula for innovating, learning, and growing—and it seemed to work. In no time at all, with a little help from our "friends," we became comfortable with our rapidly changing world by living life to the fullest, exploring everything around us, and finding our places amidst the crowd. In a world filled with so much complexity, we have always known what it takes to prosper. The trick has always been to use the special gifts we were endowed with as small children.

Living, Exploring, and Belonging

The beginning of this book set out a straightforward equation for childhood growth and development, and suggested that it was also the right formula for business success. This equation was

$$growth = living + exploring + belonging$$

As small kids we grew and prospered because we engaged the world very differently than adults did; we explored and tested everything around us, and we worked hard to belong and make a real difference. As adults in companies, we need to do the same things. That's where the thirteen special gifts fit in. When we were children, we used these gifts to become the masters of our ever-changing universe. We didn't wait for the world to come to us, but we tackled its challenges and opportunities head-on. While adults and companies talked about being more proactive, we knew there was no substitute for being consistently active, and these gifts gave us the innate ability to do whatever it took to get things done, create excitement and focus, learn and innovate, and get involved in meaningful ways.

But somewhere between the world of the sandbox and the world of business, we lost the knack. So let's pause for a moment to refresh our memories about the thirteen special gifts so we can get back to rediscovering the real keys to business success.

1. *The Gift of Play*. As kids our job was to play and constantly make things happen. As adults in companies, we need to make play and laughter important parts of our work in getting the right things done.

2. *The Gift of Enthusiasm and Energy*. As kids we were filled with endless enthusiasm, energy, and passion for anything worth doing. As adults in companies, we need to create greater enthusiasm, energy, and passion for our customers, employees, and shareholders.

3. *The Gift of Focus*. As kids we were always focused on where we were going and why we were going there. As adults in companies, we need to stay focused on our direction and be willing to ask for help along the way.

4. *The Gift of Urgency.* As kids we felt compelling urgency for anything important to us. As adults in companies, we need to understand what is really important and how to beat the clock in order to get the right things done.

5. *The Gift of Leadership.* As kids we took the lead in helping others to create their own magic. As adults in companies, we need to rediscover how to create environments where magic is an everyday occurrence.

6. *The Gift of Wonder.* As kids we found wonder in everything around us. As adults in companies, we need to rediscover wonder and possibilities in the big picture and the details of business life.

7. *The Gift of Curiosity.* As kids we looked at the world with curiosity and a burning desire to figure out how things worked. As adults in companies, we need to be much more curious about how things work, why we do them, and how to consistently improve the right things.

8. *The Gift of Questioning.* As kids we asked a million great questions. As adults in companies, we need to ask tough questions and answer them in ways that delight our customers and our people.

9. *The Gift of Trying.* As kids we tried new things without fear of failure. As adults in companies, we need to be open to trying new things, despite the chance of failure, and be more skillful in learning from our mistakes on the road to getting things right.

10. *The Gift of Creativity and Innovation.* As kids we always came up with new ideas by making many new and powerful connections. As adults in companies, we need to rediscover how to think creatively and innovate in all aspects of what we do.

11. *The Gift of Participation.* As kids we figured out how to get involved and make contributions. As adults in companies, we need to figure out how to gain the participation and unique talents of all of our people.

12. *The Gift of Cozy Places.* As kids we created safe and comfortable places where we could be our best. As adults in companies, we need to create places to safely and comfortably nurture people and their ideas.

13. *The Gift of Accomplishment.* As kids we delighted in accomplishing things great and small. As adults in companies, we need to inspire all of our people to make things happen so that everyone has the opportunity to say, "I did it!"

Along the way, we also uncovered a set of important lessons from the sandbox. The big ones were

- You can only do really good work if you enjoy what you are doing.
- Enthusiasm about something worth doing is powerful and contagious.
- It is important to know where you are going and why you want to go there.
- Matters of the greatest importance require urgency and persistence.

- Leaders create the context in which real magic happens.
- We can only reach our full potential when we start to see a world filled with wonder and possibilities.
- We can only reach our full potential when we start to scratch beneath the surface of things worth understanding.
- We can only learn and grow if we are willing to ask a lot of good questions.
- We can only learn and grow if we are willing to try new things.
- Creativity is the one key to making a real difference.
- When we have a chance to participate and use our special gifts, we can do amazing things.
- Cozy and comfortable places are the best spots for creating magic.
- Nothing is more powerful than the gift of accomplishment.

Their simple translations are in Figure 24. There is nothing very complicated about them. They were the rules of the sandbox, the playground, or anyplace else where we hung out our shingles and set up shop. They were the guidelines we used to determine how each day would be spent on our nonstop journey to learning, growing up, and creating magical results. They should be our guidelines today for building companies that learn, grow, innovate, and create magical results.

So Let's Get Started

Can you imagine what it must have been like to be the first person to paddle a canoe through the Grand Canyon, fly into space, look into a diamond, see an elephant, taste a raspberry, or climb

---

Figure 24. Lessons from the Sandbox

Play!
Be enthusiastic!
Know where you're going!
Focus on the essential things!
Help others to create magic!
Imagine a world of possibilities!
Take everything apart!
Ask a million questions!
Try new things!
Make new connections!
Get involved!
Get comfortable!
Make it happen!

---

to the summit of Mount Everest and stand on top of the world? How amazing and awe-inspiring it must have been to experience something so brand-new and full of wonder that it took your breath away. Rare and remarkable events in the world of adults. Everyday occurrences in the lives of small children.

Today and in the future, the success of companies will hinge on their ability to create an environment where rare and remarkable events become everyday occurrences for their customers, employees, partners, and shareholders—and on their ability to rediscover the gifts everyone had as small children. So get started by closing your eyes and imagining that you and your company are climbing to the summit of Mount Everest or to the very top of your industry—and all you have taken with you are thirteen special gifts, plenty of water, and a large jar of homemade salsa. Let the fun begin.

> *Everything comes to him who hustles*
> *while he waits.*
>
> THOMAS EDISON

A Note for Working Parents

One of the great struggles for most working parents is the need to balance work and family. We are told by the world around us that these are two distinct and separate parts of our lives. At best, we try to find places to work that are understanding and somewhat flexible in giving us time to attend to the major priorities in our personal lives. At worst, however, we constantly battle to be good-enough employees and good-enough parents. In other words, we try to do OK at two things that are both very important to us.

As you have gathered from this book, it doesn't have to be this way. While the primary theme of this book is that we can be more successful in business by rediscovering the gifts we had as kids, working parents should get an equally important message: We can be more successful in business not just by making time for our children and families but by interacting with and learning from our kids. This has profound implications for us and our companies. Spending time with our children provides powerful and consistent guidance for us as we work to rediscover and master the thirteen special gifts. After all, children are the living and breathing embodiments of what it takes to learn, grow, and prosper. Given this, it should be in our best interest, and the best interest of our companies, to encourage us to spend time learning from and with our children.

If you would like more information on how to help your company tap the wisdom and magic of childhood, feel free to visit www.lessonsfromthesandbox.com.

Concluding Note

While every child is born with the special gifts described in this book, many children in our society and societies around the world have little chance to delight in the magic of childhood. Whether due to poverty, sickness, famine, or war, they live in places where simply surviving takes precedence over living, exploring, and belonging—where opportunies to wonder, imagine, question, try, and innovate rarely come along.

There is a lot that all of us can do, as companies and as individuals, to make a difference in the lives of children in need. In our communities, we can begin by taking the time to read with or mentor a child at a local school. If you are not doing this already, you will be surprised by how much you can offer with a small amount of your time and how much you will gain that will enrich your personal and business lives. If there is another powerful lesson in this book it is this: Unlocking the magic in a child is probably the best way to unlock the magic in you.

To find ideas and information on how you can make a difference, visit www.lessonsfromthesandbox.com.

Testing Your IQ

This test is designed to provide a snapshot of your company's ability to think and act like a small child in order to learn, grow, and thrive. While it is not a completely scientific assessment, it can help you to identify those areas in which you can rediscover some of the magic you had as a small child.

Instructions

Answer each question by scoring
  3 points for "Yes"
  2 points for "Almost"
  1 point for "Not exactly"
  0 points for "We're clueless"

The Questions

1. Are people in the organization encouraged to play and have fun in support of key business objectives?

2. Are laughter and spontaneity part of the culture?

3. Are your people enthusiastic about your products and services and the value you provide to customers?

4. Is there a high level of energy in the organization?

5. Does your company have a clear vision and strategy, and is it communicated effectively to all employees?

6. Are employees encouraged to ask senior management about the direction of the company and what they can do to help?

7. Is there a compelling urgency for doing the most important things?

8. Does the company give employees guidance and support in beating the clock?

9. Does senior management focus attention on the importance of innovation as a key to growth?

10. Does senior management identify and eliminate barriers that prevent employees from doing new and worthwhile things?

11. Are people across the organization challenged and encouraged to wonder and to imagine possibilities for dramatically changing the business?

12. Are people given opportunities to explore a world of ideas, including other companies' best practices, and things found in museums and nature?

13. Are people across the organization challenged and encouraged to figure out ways to constantly improve products, services, and all aspects of the business?

14. Are people encouraged to question anything about the company?

15. Are people encouraged to try new things even though they might not work out?

16. Are people given the time and resources to develop new ideas and innovations?

17. Are people given training and coaching in how to think creatively?

18. Are there appropriate incentives to spur innovation and risk-taking?

19. Does the company do a good job of tapping the talents and perspectives of all of its people?

20. Does the company encourage people to create cozy places for being at their best?

21. Does the company make a concerted effort to acknowledge and reward people for trying to make a difference?

Scoring

Use this scale to gauge your Sandbox IQ:

50–63 = You are well on your way to thinking and growing like a child.

35–49 = You have already rediscovered many of the gifts and are getting results.

20–34 = You understand the importance of the gifts and have made a start.

0–19 = You have not lost all of your childhood abilities.

Great Things to Read

One way to rediscover the magic of childhood is to read a great children's book. Here are some of our customers' and our favorites. In addition to being among the finest stories written (and illustrated) for any age, each of these books has some important clues to business success. You can read them by yourself for the sheer delight of it or use them with your team members as the starting point for acting on an important opportunity or challenge.

A Chair for My Mother by Vera Williams. Greenwillow, 1984.

Charlotte's Web by E. B. White. Harper Collins Publishers, 1952.

Comet in Moominland by Tove Jansson (translated by Elizabeth Portch). Farrar, Straus and Giroux, 1951.

Curious George Goes to the Hospital by Margret and H. A. Rey. Houghton Mifflin Company, 1966.

Doctor De Soto by William Steig. Scholastic Books, 1982.

If I Ran the Zoo by Dr. Seuss. Random House, 1966.

Lilly's Purple Plastic Purse by Kevin Henkes. Greenwillow, 1996.

The Little Engine That Could retold by Watty Piper. Platt & Munk Publishers, 1930.

Make Way For Ducklings by Robert McCloskey. Viking Press, 1941.

Mother Goose: A Collection of Classic Nursery Rhymes illustrated by Michael Hague. Henry Holt & Company, 1988.

Mufaro's Beautiful Daughters: An African Tale by John Steptoe (translated by Clarita Kohen). Lothrop Lee & Shepard, 1987.

Nate the Great by Marjorie Weinman Sharmat. Coward, McCann & Geoghegan, Inc., 1972.

The Phantom Tollbooth by Norton Juster. Alfred A. Knopf, 1961.

Pippi Longstocking by Astrid Lindgren (translated by Florence Lamborn). Viking Press, 1950.

Raising Dragons by Jerdine Nolen. Silver Whistle Press, 1998.

Snowflake Bentley by Jacqueline Briggs Martin. Houghton Mifflin Company, 1998.

Somewhere in the World Right Now by Stacey Schuett. Dragonfly Press, 1997.

Stuart Little by E. B. White. Harper & Row Publishers, 1945.

The Tortoise and the Hare adapted by Janet Stevens from the original Aesop fable. Holiday House, 1984.

The Velveteen Rabbit by Margery Williams. Doubleday, 1922.

Verdi by Janell Cannon. Harcourt Brace, 1997.

Where the Sidewalk Ends by Shel Silverstein. Harper Collins Publishers, 1974.

Where the Wild Things Are by Maurice Sendak. Harper Collins Publishers, 1963.

"Wynken, Blynken and Nod" by Eugene Field. From *Poems of Childhood*, Airmont Publishing Company (1894), reissued 1969.

About the Author

Dr. Alan S. Gregerman is the founder and President of VENTURE WORKS Inc., and a renowned authority on business strategy and innovation. During the past twelve years he has helped over 300 teams create winning strategies and important innovations—with a 90 percent success rate. He is also an award-winning teacher, public speaker, and facilitator who has been called "the most creative person in the Mid-Atlantic" and "the Robin Williams of business consulting." His customers include a wide range of growing companies, entrepreneurial start-ups, and Fortune 500 firms such as GTE, Discovery Communications, SmithKline Beecham, Marriott, and Nortel Networks.

Dr. Gregerman earned his B.A. in geography from Northwestern University and his M.A. in economic geography and Ph.D. in urban and technological planning from the University of Michigan in Ann Arbor. He recently served as the first visiting scholar in entrepreneurship and economic growth at the U.S. Congressional Research Service. In his free time, Gregerman is president of the board of the Human Services Institute where he is involved in efforts to break down barriers that separate people with disabilities from leading "normal" everyday lives. He lives outside Washington, D.C., with his wife and three children.

For more information on VENTURE WORKS, please feel free to contact us at:

VENTURE WORKS Inc.
Corporate Headquarters:
1210 Woodside Parkway
Silver Spring, Maryland 20910 U.S.A.
www.venture-works.com
Phone: (301) 585-1600
E-mail: innovate@venture-works.com